Classic Duologues
For Female Actors

ISBN: 9798599255086

DEDICATION

This collection of acting duologues for female actors is dedicated to all teachers and students of drama with a love of performing from the classics. These scenes are suitable for a wide range of study, performance, auditions, exams and festivals.

ACKNOWLEDGEMENTS

A special thanks goes to my husband Steve, who has prepared this collection for publication, and has bailed me out on numerous occasions over the years, with his technical expertise.

TABLE OF CONTENTS

INTRODUCTION

I have compiled and edited this collection of Classic duologues for female actors to study, perform and enjoy. These scenes are suitable for a range of acting exams and awards as well as for auditions and festivals. I have tried and tested these scenes with numerous students over the years with great success and more importantly, they have thoroughly enjoyed working on them

The duologues in this collection are taken from a range of plays including works from the Greeks, Restoration Drama, French Farce, Ibsen, Chekhov, Wilde, Shaw, Tennessee Williams and Jean Anouilh. Each scene has an introduction prepared suitable for exam or festival work and are also timed with exams and festival work in mind. I hope you enjoy this collection.

DUO ACTING

Duo acting involves two actors and therefore it is essential to build up a rapport with the person you are going to be acting with. A trust and confidence in each other is essential and it will be necessary to find time to rehearse together as well as apart. It is equally important to choose a scene which suits both players and which has a balanced amount of text for each speaker, where possible. It is preferable for each actor to play only one role. Duo acting is great fun and is a good way of learning to share and communicate with each other.

Duologues are extremely rewarding as well as useful to work on with students in drama classes and most examination boards and drama festivals offer a range of duo acting examinations. There is a wide range of classical material in this book aimed at stimulating and stretching the actor. I have provided a useful introduction to the scenes and limited stage directions. I believe the actor will work towards understanding the scene within the context of the play as a whole and work creatively towards staging these scenes in their own unique way.

ACTING A ROLE

When preparing for acting a role one should always study the play as a whole if you can and approach your chosen scene in context within the whole play.

Here are some questions to consider:

Is your character a central character or a leading

character? Is your character crucial to the development

of the plot?

Or is your character a stock character or small cameo

role, providing a sub-plot, comedy or light relief to the plot?

What does your character look like in terms of physical appearance? This can be considered in terms of age, height, physique, posture, colouring etc.

How do you envisage your character in costume? Do you need to consider the historical period for your chosen role and research the type of costume you would be wearing?

Think about how you might like to play your character in terms of physical and vocal skills? Is your natural voice appropriate or do you need to characterise your voice and speak with an accent or dialect?

How does your character develop throughout the play? Try to map your character's journey throughout the play? What are your character's likes, dislikes? How do you relate to your character and how does your character relate to the other characters in the play?

What do you like about your character? Try to create a backstory for your character.

What is your character's role/purpose in the play? Try to establish his/her objective within the scene you are playing or even in the play as a whole.

Consider casting. Is this role a good choice for you? Does this character suit your acting skills and personality?

What skills and characteristics do you need as an actor to play this character?

ACTING STYLE

It is important to adopt the correct style of acting for your chosen performance piece. You will need to consider whether your scene is perhaps from the realist school of writing, or whether you are performing Shakespeare and need to acquire knowledge of the metre which Shakespeare writes in. Or perhaps you have chosen a piece which relies purely on fantasy and imagination. These are all choices you will have to consider when tackling a scene.

Fantasy

This style of acting has no limitations. In fantasy, anything can happen in fantasy stories and the actor has great scope to use their imagination. This style is not to be taken too seriously and offers the actor great creativity. The style of acting is often larger than life and 'overacting' in these types of roles is common and acceptable.

Comedy and Tragedy

It is necessary to identify the genre of your play as this will affect your playing style. Good timing is essential in comedy and many roles will require a heightened use of realism to create the desired comic effect. However, if you are playing tragedy, a more serious and sombre acting style will be required. There are many styles of acting and these need to be identified and an appropriate playing style adopted, according to the writing style of your chosen play.

Realism

Realism, is a literary technique which describes locations, characters and themes in a realistic style without using elaborate imagery or rhetorical language. This means that the emotions of the characters have to be sincere and believable.

Playing the Objective

The Theatre Practitioner, Constantine Stanislavski, suggested that a whole play be separated into a series of smaller scenes or units of performance. In each unit there will be an objective. The objectives from these units will form or lead to a Super objective.

Basically, playing the objective means identifying what your character is trying to achieve in each scene? What is your character's motivation? If this goal can be established, the performer will have discovered an overall objective.

When analyzing a play, you should look for its' overall aim or theme. The scenes can be broken up into parts. Decide on the objective for each scene or unit. Ideally, the objective should be considered as a verb, an action; something your character ideally wants to do or achieve

The Super-Objective

It helps to work out what the super-objective of the play is, as a whole. It must be the fundamental driving force of the whole play. The super objective is easy to determine in a well-written play. The objective should be described in terms of a verb. The "through line of action" must guide everything towards the super objective.

Period

You should be aware of the period of the writing style and consider the manners which were used during this time. This also means considering the costumes worn during the period.

Truth

The actor should always aim to perform with truth, imagination and sincerity. Spontaneity in acting and is key in order to convince your audience of your credibility.

DUOLOGUES

ANCIENT GREEK THEATRE & LITERATURE

The Greek Empire began in the 8th Century BC and fell in the 4th Century BC. It was during this period that theatre originated. Ancient Greek theatre flourished, and from this, three genres emerged, tragedy, which emerged during the late 6th century BC, comedy, 486 BC and the satyr play. Theatre developed from a festival during the grape harvesting time, which the Greeks celebrated in honour of the God Dionysus. This eventually turned into a playwriting competition, and it was for festivals like these that most of the Ancient literature we have today was written for. Theatre was extremely important in Ancient Greek Civilisation. To signify the importance of this event, the high-status Olympic Champions, were given the privilege of the best seats in the theatre. The sheer size of the open air amphitheatres is extraordinary, some holding 15,000 people. These theatres were either semi-circular or entirely circular, providing fantastic acoustics. There was an orchestra, where the Chorus usually stood, and a skene which was a backdrop and was also a place for the actors to change. Little is known about the acting styles in Greek theatre. There was no fourth wall. Like the chorus, the actors could see the audience, and would have spoken directly to them. The actors' masks were quite sophisticated and had megaphones built into the mouths of their masks to amplify their voices.

Greece's poetic movement was one of the key literary movements of Ancient Greece during the period between the 7th and 4th centuries BC. It was during this movement that poetry was being written down for the first time, and in many forms, for example, the ode, epic, tragedy, comedy, therefore making this one of the greatest and revolutionary movements in world history. It ended when Greece was conquered by Rome, and the Republican period began.

Ancient theatre is known for the wearing of masks and allowed those seated at the back of the theatre to see the expressions of the characters. This therefore meant that the audience knew the characters' age, sex, status and also how they should react and respond towards the characters. For the Chorus of the play, the masks created unity, representing a many-voiced persona. Just like group speaking today. Furthermore, masks allowed the all-male cast to play female characters convincingly, while also heightening the emotions of the audience. This use of masks has inspired many modern theatre styles, particularly Commedia dell Arte, which relies on physical movement and masks to portray the characters to the audience.

The Ancient Greeks wore long flowing tunics and boots called *cothurni*, worn by those playing tragic roles. These boots elevated them above the other actors. The actors with comedic roles only wore a thin-soled shoe called a sock. These both clearly symbolized the roles of each actor, whilst also ensuring the audience members at the back of the theatre could follow the plot, by visually representing the mood of each scene.

The Chorus, a common part of an Ancient play, consisted of between 12 and 50 players, <u>Aeschylus</u> lowered the number to twelve, and <u>Sophocles</u> raised it again to fifteen. The group was led by the choryphaeus who was the main member of the Chorus. They often danced, sang and spoke their lines in unison, commenting on the action of the performance. They helped to offer context and summarized the performance.

Most Ancient poetry or prose is written in dactylic hexameter. This rhythm consists of one long syllable followed by two shorter syllables, having the rhythm **dum** de de, **dum** de de, **dum** de de **dum** de de, **dum** de de, **dum** de de. Hexameter indicates that this rhythm is repeated six times per line. The translations of the Ancient literature which we read now-a-days, no longer has this rhythm. It is often translated into prose. The Ancient drama dialogue is written in iambic trimeter, which consists of one unstressed syllable followed by one stressed syllable, de/**dum** de/**dum** de/**dum**. Trimeter means that this is repeated three times per line. The Chorus' lines are instead written in choral lyric, suggesting that they were sung instead of spoken.

Euripides
Euripides was a Greek playwright living between 480-406 BC. Euripides is known as one of the three greatest tragedians, along

with Aeschylus and Sophocles. Although he has this title today, he was unappreciated during his life, winning just four awards, in comparison to Sophocles' twenty. This is because Euripides was known as a leader of 'corrupt views', challenging the state with his writing. He and many others competed in the dramatic festival of Dionysus, and it was here where Euripides was ridiculed. The comic playwright, Aristophanes, scripted Euripides as a foolish character in three of his plays, publicly humiliating him. Euripides was a rather eccentric man, having been married twice, yet both wives having been unfaithful. He became a recluse, and lived in a cave on the island of Salamis. Despite this, Euripides influenced modern theatre drastically, as he represented mythical heroes as ordinary people in extraordinary circumstances. He therefore became known as 'the most tragic of poets' as he focused on the inner lives and motives of characters, adding more depth to the stock two-dimensional characters of myths. Euripides' most famous works include *Medea*, *Trojan Women* and *The Bacchae*. *Medea* was rather unpopular at the time, due to his inclusions of dragons, which was considered untraditional and ridiculous. Furthermore, Euripides portrays the character of Medea as sympathetic whereas Jason appears cowardly. This would have been unpopular among his contemporary audiences which consisted mostly of men.

Sophocles

Sophocles lived between the years 496 and 406 BC, Sophocles remains one of the greatest influencers of drama. An example of his innovations is his addition of a third actor, which further reduced the role of the <u>chorus</u> and created greater opportunity for character development and conflict between characters. This was an interest of Sophocles', as he was more concerned with a characters' struggle with fate and character development. Sophocles won more competitions than both of his contemporary tragic writers, enjoying a total of at least 18 wins. It is thought that Sophocles wrote at least 123 plays, only 7 of which have survived, the most famous being *Antigone*, *Oedipus Rex* and *Ajax*. *Antigone* and *Oedipus Rex* are part of a trilogy following the misfortunes of King Oedipus who married his mother, and upon discovering the truth, blinded himself. *Antigone* focuses on the fate of his daughter after his death, as she is faced with the choice of obeying the law of the king of the land and leave her brother's body to remain unburied, or to obey the law of the gods. She decides to bury her brother, and is, as a result, sentenced to death. The complex concepts of right and wrong, punishment and reward are present throughout Sophocles' writing, indicating that the choices made by characters were of interest to him.

ANTIGONE BY SOPHOCLES (441 BC)

(Antigone is informing her younger sister, Ismene, that she intends to defy their uncle King Creon and bury her brother, Polynices. Polynices has been left to rot whilst their elder brother has been dignified with a decent burial).

Antigone:
Own sister of my blood, one life with me,
Ismene, have the tidings caught thy ear?
Say, hath not Heaven decreed to execute
on thee and me, while yet we are alive,
all the evil Oedipus bequeathed? All horror,
all pain, all outrage, falls on us! And now
the General's proclamation of to-day –
Hast thou not heard? – Art thou so slow to hear
when harm from foes threatens the souls we love?

Ismene:
No word of those we love, Antigone,
painful or glad, hath reached me, since we two
were utterly deprived of our two brothers,
cut off with mutual stroke, both in one day
and since the Argive host this now-past night
is vanished, I know nought beside to make me
nearer to happiness or more in woe.

Antigone:
I knew it well, and therefore let thee forth
the palace gate that thou alone might'st hear.

Ismene:
Speak on. Thy troubled look bodes some dark news.

Antigone:
Why, hath not Creon, in the burial-rite,
of our two brethren honoured one, and wrought
on one foul wrong? Eteocles, they tell,
with lawful consecration he lays out,
and after covers him in earth, adorned

with amplest honours in the world below.
But Polynices, miserably slain.
They say tis publicly proclaimed that none
must cover in a grave, nor mourn for him'
but leave him tombless and unwept, a store
of sweet provision for the carrion fowl
that eye him greedily. Such a righteous law
Good Creon hath pronounced for thy behoof –
Ay, and for mine! I am not left out! – And now
he moves this way to promulgate his will
to such as have not heard, nor lightly holds
the thing he bids, but whoso disobeys,
the citizens shall stone him to the death.
This is the matter, and thou wilt quickly show
if thou art noble, or fallen below they birth.

Ismene:
Unhappy one! But what can I herein
avail to do or undo?

Antigone:
Wilt thou share
the danger and the labour? Make thy choice.

Ismene:
Of what wild enterprise? What canst thou mean?

Antigone:
Wilt thou join hand with mine to lift the dead?

Ismene:
To bury him when all have been forbidden?
Is that thy thought?

Antigone:
To bury my own brother
And thine, even though you wilt not do thy part.
I will not be a traitress to my kin.

—

Ismene:
Fool-hardy girl against the word of Creon?

Antigone:
He hath no right to bar me from mine own.

Ismene:
Ah, sister, think but how our father fell,
hated of all and lost to fair renown,
through self-detected crimes, - with his own hand,
self-wreaking how he dashed out both his eyes:
then how the mother wife, sad two-fold name,
with twisted halter bruised her life away.
Last, how in one dire moment our two brothers
with internecine conflict at one blow
wrought out by fratricide their mutual doom.
Now, left alone, O think how beyond all
most piteously we twain shall be destroyed,
if in defiance of authority
we traverse the commandment of the King!
We needs but bear in mind we are but women,
never created to contend with men;
nay more, made victims of resistless power,
to obey behests more harsh than this today.
I, then, imploring those beneath to grant
indulgence, seeing I am enforced in this,
will yield submission to the powers that rule,
small wisdom were it to overpass the bound.

Antigone:
I will not urge you. Nor if now you list
to help me, will your help afford me joy.
Be what you choose to be. This single hand
shall bury our lost brother. Glorious
for me to take this labour and die.
Dear to him will my soul be as we rest
in death, when I have dared this holy crime.
My time for pleasing men will soon be over;
not so my duty toward the Dead. My home
yonder will have no end. You, if you will,

May pour contempt on laws revered on High.

Ismene:
Not from irreverence. But I have no strength
to strive against the citizens' resolve.

Antigone:
Thou, make excuses! I will go my way
to raise a burial-mound to my dear brother.

Ismene:
O hapless maiden, how I fear for thee.

Antigone:
Waste not your fears on me. Guide your own fortune.

Ismene:
Ah, yet divulge thin enterprise to none,
but keep the secret close, and so will I.

Antigone:
I know that I please those whom I would please.
Fate cannot rob me of a noble death.

THE PHOENICIAN WOMEN BY EURIPIDES
(409 BC)

(Set in Thebes. Jocasta and Oedipus's two sons, Eteocles and Polynices battle against each other to take control of the city. Jocasta and her daughter Antigone are concerned. Jocasta wants to stop them from killing each other. Unfortunately, she is unable to do so and later when she discovers their bodies, she kills herself).

Jocasta:
My child Antigone, come outside the house.
No help for you in maidens' works and dances.
The gods have set it so. But those brave men
Your brothers, who are rushing in their death,
You and your mother must keep from mutual murder.

Antigone:
Mother, what new terror for your own
Do you cry out before the palace front?

Jocasta:
Daughter, your brothers' lives are falling fast.

Antigone:
What do you say?

Jocasta:
They're set for single fight.

Antigone:
What will you tell me?

Jocasta:
Hard words. Follow me.

Antigone:
Where, as I leave my chamber?

Jocasta:
To the armies.

Antigone:
I fear the crowd.

Jocasta:
Modesty will not help.

Antigone:
What shall I do?

Jocasta:
Undo your brothers' strife.

Antigone:
But how?

Jocasta:
Prostrate, with me, before them.

Antigone:
Lead, Mother, to the plain. We can't delay.

Jocasta:
Then hurry, hurry, daughter. If I catch them
Before they hurl their spears, my life's in light.
But if they die, I'll lie with them in death.

ELECTRA BY EURIPIDES
(412 BC)

(Electra, the daughter of Clytemnestra are arguing over Clytemnestra's former husband Agamemnon's murder. Clytemnestra is now married to Aegisthus. Electra seeks revenge for her father).

Clytemnestra:
Get out of the carriage, Trojan maidens; hold my hand tight,
so I can step down safely to the ground.
Mostly we gave the houses of our gods the spoils
From Phrygia, but these girls, the best in Troy, I chose
To ornament my own house and replace the child
I lost, my loved daughter. The compensation is small.

Electra:
Then may not I, who am a slave and also tossed
Far from my father's home to live in misery,
May I not, Mother, hold your most distinguished hand?

Clytemnestra:
These slaves are here to help me. Do not trouble yourself.

Electra:
Why not? You rooted me up, a casualty of war;
My home was overpowered; I am in your power,
As they are too – left dark, lonely, and fatherless.

Clytemnestra:
And dark and lonely were your father's plots against
Those he should most have loved and least conspired to kill.
I can tell you – no. When a woman gets an evil
Reputation she finds a bitter twist to her words.
This is my case now, not a pretty one. And yet,
If you have something truly to hate, you ought to learn
The facts first; then hate is more decent. But not in the dark.
I was unfairly wronged, yet not for this

Would I have gone savage so, nor killed my husband so,
But he came home to me with a mad, god-filled girl
And introduced her to our bed. So, there we were,
Two brides being stabled in a single stall.
The dirty gossip puts us in the spotlight;
The guilty ones, the men, are never blamed at all.
I killed. I turned and walked the only path still open,
Straight to his enemies. Would any of his friends
Have helped me in the task of murder I had to do?
Speak if you have need or reason. Fight me free;
Demonstrate how your father died without full justice.

Electra:
Keep in mind, Mother, those last words you spoke,
Giving me license to speak out freely against you.

Clytemnestra:
I say them once again, child; I will not deny you.

Electra:
But when you hear me, Mother, will you hurt me again?

Clytemnestra:
Not so at all. I shall be glad to humour you.

Electra:
You, long before your daughter came near sacrifice,
The very hour your husband marched away from home,
Were setting your brown curls by the bronze mirror's light.
Now any woman who works on her beauty when her man
Is gone from home indicts herself as being a whore.
She has no decent cause to show her painted face
Outside the door unless she wants to look for trouble.
Next, if, as you say, our father killed your daughter,
Did I do any harm to you, or did my brother?
When you killed your husband, why did you not bestow
The ancestral home on us, but took to bed the gold
Which never belonged to you to buy yourself a lover?
And why has he not gone in exile for your son
Or died to pay for me who still alive have died

My sister's death twice over while you strangle my life?
If murder judges and calls for murder, I will kill
You – and your own Orestes will kill you – for Father.
If the first death was just, the second too is just.

Clytemnestra:
My child, from birth you always have adored your father.
This is part of life. Some children always love
The male, some turn more closely to their mother than him.
I know you and forgive you. I am not so happy
Either, child, with what I have done or with myself.
O god, how miserably my plans have all turned out.
Perhaps I drove my hate too hard against my husband.

Electra:
Your mourning comes a little late. There is no cure.
Father is dead now. If you grieve, why not
Recall the son you sent to starve in foreign lands?

Clytemnestra:
I am afraid. I have to watch my life, not his.
They say his father's death has made him very angry.

Electra:
Why do you let your husband act like a beast against us?

Clytemnestra:
That is his nature. Yours is wild and stubborn too.

Electra:
That hurts. But I am going to bury my anger soon.

Clytemnestra:
Good; then he never will be harsh to you again.

Electra:
He has been haughty; now he is staying in my house.

Clytemnestra:
You see? You want to blow the quarrel to new flames.

Electra:
I will be quiet; I fear him – the way I fear him.

Clytemnestra:
Stop this talk. You called me here for something, girl.

Electra:
I think you heard about my lying-in and son.
Make me the proper sacrifice – I don't know how –
As the law runs for children at the tenth night moon.
I have no knowledge; I never had a family.

Clytemnestra:
This is work for the woman who acted as your midwife.

Electra:
I acted for myself. I was alone at birth.

Clytemnestra:
Your house is set so desolate of friends and neighbours?

Electra:
No one is willing to make friends with poverty.

Clytemnestra:
Then I will go and make the gods full sacrifice
For a child as law prescribes. I give you so much
Grace and then pass to the meadow where my husband rests
Praying to the bridal Nymphs. Servants, take the wagon,
Set it in the stables. When you think this rite
Of god draws to an end, come back to stand beside me,
For I have debts of grace to pay my husband too.

Electra:
Enter our poor house. And, Mother, take good care
The smoky walls put no dark stain upon your robes.
Pay sacrifice to heaven as you ought to pay.
(Clytemnestra walks alone into the house).
The basket of grain is raised again, the knife is sharp
Which killed the bull, and close beside him you shall fall

Stricken, to keep your bridal rites in the house of death
With him you slept beside in life. I give you so
Much grace and you shall give my father grace of justice.

MEDEA BY EURIPIDES
(431BC)

(Medea's husband, Jason, is to remarry. Medea is furious. The children's nurse tries to console her and pleads for the children's innocence in the whole affair).

<u>Medea:</u>
Ah, wretch! Ah, lost in my sufferings,
I wish, I wish I might die.

<u>Nurse:</u> *(talking to Medea's children).*
What did I say, dear children? Your mother
Frets her heart and frets it to anger.
Run away quickly into the house,
And keep well out of her sight.
Don't go anywhere near, but be careful
Of the wildness and bitter nature
Of that proud mind.
O now! Run quickly indoors.
Go now! Run quickly indoors.
It is clear that she soon will put lightning
In that cloud of her cries that is rising
With a passion increasing. O, what will she do,
Proud-hearted and not to be checked on her course,
A soul bitten into with wrong?

(The tutor comes to take the children into the house).

<u>Medea:</u>
Ah, I have suffered
What should be wept for bitterly. I hate you,
Children of a hateful mother. I curse you
And your father. Let the whole house crash.

<u>Nurse:</u>
Ah, I pity you, you poor creature.
How can your children share in their father's
Wickedness? Why do you hate them? Oh children,
How much I fear that something may happen!

Great people's tempers are terrible, always
Having their own way, seldom checked,
Dangerous they shift from mood to mood.
How much better to have been accustomed
To live on equal terms with one's neighbours.
I would like to be safe and grow old in a
Humble way. What is moderate sounds best,
Also, in practice is best for everyone.
Greatness brings no profit to people.
God indeed, when in anger, brings
Greater ruin to great men's houses.

WILLIAM SHAKESPEARE 1564-1616
SHAKESPEARE'S WRITING STYLE

William Shakespeare, from Stratford on Avon, wrote 37 plays and 154 sonnets. The plays are loosely categorised as comedies, tragedies and histories. By the age of twenty-eight, Shakespeare was well established in London as an actor and playwright. The highly successful Globe Theatre was built in London with a capacity of 2,500-3,000. It was known as 'The Wooden O' due to its' shape. During the Elizabethan times, there were no female actresses, only male actors. The young boys played the women's parts. The actors were given only their own parts to the play. It wasn't until the 16th and 17th Century that printing became available, enabling Shakespeare's plays to be published. Printers would often change the words of a playwright's play in order for them to fit onto the published page. Shakespeare's characters are depicted as real people with universal emotions. However, one must appreciate the writing is most often in verse and therefore knowledge of the metre and style of his writing is essential.

Metre and Rhythm
English is a stress language. This means that our language is made up of strong and weak stresses. Verse is made up of these stresses set in regular patterns which is what we call METRE.
A metrical unit is called a FOOT. This comes from ancient Greece, where, in dance, the foot was raised up and down on the beat of a bar of music. A metrical line is named according to the number of feet in a line.

Iambic Pentametre
Iambic has one unstressed & one stressed syllable OR one weak syllable & one strong syllable. **Iambic Pentametre** (used by Shakespeare & other writers) is made up of 5 feet of iambic rhythms.e.g. de <u>dum</u>/de <u>dum</u>/de <u>dum</u>/de <u>dum</u>/de <u>dum</u>. e.g. 'The <u>clock</u> struck <u>nine</u> when <u>I</u> did <u>send</u> the <u>nurse</u>' and 'I <u>left</u> no <u>ring</u> with <u>her</u>, what <u>means</u> this <u>lady</u>?' Take note of the **hemi-stich**: where one character speaks half a line and the next character finishes the second half of the line. The rhythm of iambic pentameter resembles the beating of the human heart and is closest to natural rhythms of natural speech. Blank verse (verse without rhyme) is

the closest rhythm to natural speech. It has no regular rhyme and is therefore ideal for writing verse plays. There are, however, inversions and other variations which are added to create variety in the rhythm. Shakespeare often uses prose to vary his writing too. This is often reserved for the lower status characters, but not always. It is sometimes used to depict informality.

AS YOU LIKE IT ACT 3, SC 2 BY WILLIAM SHAKESPEARE (1599)

(Rosalind and Celia are now living in disguise in the Forest of Arden. Orlando, madly in love with Rosalind, has been penning verses to her and attaching them to tree trunks in the forest. Little does he know that Ganymede is indeed Rosalind in disguise. Both Rosalind and Celia have seen the verses and are greatly amused by them. This duologue is written in prose)

Celia:
Didst thou hear these verses?

Rosalind:
O yes, I heard them all, and more too; for some of them had in them more feet than the verses would bear.

Celia:
That's no matter; the feet might bear the verses.

Rosalind:
Ay, but the feet were lame, and could not bear themselves without the verse, and therefore stood lamely in the verse.

Celia:
But didst thou hear, without wondering how thy name should be hanged and carved upon these trees?

Rosalind:
I was seven of the nine days out of the wonder before you came; for look here what I found on a palm-tree. I was never so berhymed since Pythagoras' time, that I was an Irish rat, which I can hardly remember.

Celia:
Trow you who hath done this?

Rosalind:
Is it a man?

Celia:
And a chain, that you once wore, about his neck. Change you colour?

Rosalind:
I prithee, who?

Celia:
O lord, lord! It is a hard matter for friends to meet; but mountains may be removed with earthquakes, and so encounter.

Rosalind:
Nay, but who is it?

Celia:
Is it possible?

Rosalind:
Nay, I pray thee now, with most petitionary vehemence, tell me who it is.

Celia:
O wonderful, wonderful, and most wonderful wonderful, and yet again wonderful, and after that out of all whooping!

Rosalind:
Good my complexion! Dost thou think, though I am caparisoned like a man, I have a doublet and hose in my disposition? One inch of delay more is a South-sea of discovery. I prithee, tell me, who is it? Quickly, and speak apace. I would thou could'st stammer, that thou might'st pour this concealed man out of thy mouth, as wine comes out of a narrow-mouthed bottle; either too much at once, or none at all. Is he of God's making? What manner of man? Is his head worth a hat, or his chin worth a beard?

Celia:
Nay, he hath but a little beard.

Rosalind:
Why, God will send more, if the man will be thankful: let me stay

the growth of his beard, if thou delay me not the knowledge of his chin.

Celia:
It is young Orlando, that tripped up the wrestler's heels, and your heart, both in an instant.

Rosalind:
Nay, but no mocking; speak sad brow and true maid.

Celia:
I'faith, coz, 'tis he.

Rosalind:
Orlando?

Celia:
Orlando.

Rosalind:
Alas the day! What shall I do with my doublet and hose? What did he when thou saw'st him? What said he? How looked he? Wherein went he? What makes he here? Did he ask for me? Where remains he? How parted he with thee? And when shalt thou see him again? – Answer me in one word.

Celia:
You must borrow me Gargantua's mouth first: 'tis a word too great for any mouth of this age's size. To say "Ay" and "No' to these particulars, is more than to answer in a catechism.

Rosalind:
But doth he know that I am in this forest, and in man's apparel? Looks he as freshly as he did the day he wrestled?

Celia:
It is as easy to count atomies as to resolve the propositions of a lover: but take a taste of my finding him, and relish it with a good observance. I found him under a tree, like a dropped acorn.

Rosalind:
It may well be called Jove's tree, when it drops forth such fruit.

Celia:
Give me audience, good madam.

Rosalind:
Proceed.

Celia:
There lay he, stretched along, like a wounded knight.

Rosalind:
Though it be pity to see such sight, it well becomes the ground.

Celia:
Cry, holla! To thy tongue, I prithee; it curvets unseasonably. He was furnished like a hunter.

Rosalind:
O ominous! He comes to kill my heart.

Celia:
I would sing my song without a burden: thou bring'st me out of tune.

Rosalind:
Do you not know I am a woman? When I think, I must speak. Sweet, say on.

Celia:
You bring me out, - Soft! Comes he not here!

Rosalind:
'T is he: slink by, and note him.

TWELFTH NIGHT ACT 3 SC 1 (1602)
BY WILLIAM SHAKESPEARE

(Viola, dressed as a male messenger named Cesario pays a second visit to the Countess Oliva, who has fallen in love with him and has no interest whatsoever in Viola's master, the Duke Orsino).

Olivia:
Let the garden door be shut, and leave me to my hearing.
(To Viola) Give me your hand, sir.

Viola:
My duty, madam, and most humble service.

Olivia:
What is your name?

Viola:
Cesario is your servants name, fair princess.

Olivia:
My servant, sir? 'Twas never merry world
Since lowly feigning was call'd compliment:
You are servant to the Count Orsino, youth.

Viola:
And he is yours, and his must needs be yours:
Your servant's servant is our servant, madam.

Olivia:
For him, I think not on him: For his thoughts,
Would they were blanks, rather than fill'd with me.

Viola:
Madam, I come to whet your gentle thoughts
On his behalf.

Olivia:
              O, by your leave, I pray you!

I bade you never speak again of him;
But would you undertake another suit,
I had rather hear you solicit that,
Thank music from the spheres.

Viola:

Dear lady –

Olivia:
Give me leave, beseech you. I did send,
After the last enchantment you did here,
A ring in chase of you. So, did I abuse
Myself, my servant, and, I fear me, you.
Under your hard construction must I sit,
To force that on you in a shameful cunning
Which you knew none of yours. What might you think?
Have you not set mine honour at the stake,
And baited it with all th'unmuzzled thoughts
That tyrannous heart can think? To one of your receiving
Enough is shown; a cypress, not a bosom
Hides my heart: So, let me hear you speak.

Viola:
I pity you.

Olivia:
That's a degree to love.

Viola:
No, not a grize: for 'tis a vulgar proof
That very oft we pity enemies.

Olivia:
Why then methinks 'tis time to smile again.
O world, how apt the poor are to be proud!
If one should be a prey, how much better
to fall before the lion than the wolf! *(Olivia hears the clock striking)*.
The clock upbraids me with the waste of time,
Be not afraid, good youth, I will not have you,
And yet when wit and youth is come to harvest,

—

Your wife is like to reap a proper man.
There lies your way, due west.

Viola:

Then westward ho!
Grace and good deposition attend your ladyship!
You'll nothing, madam, to my lord by me?

Olivia:
Stay!
I prithee tell me what thou think'st of me.

Viola:
That you do not think you are not what you are.

Olivia:
If I think so, I think the same of you.

Viola:
Then think you right; I am not what I am.

Olivia:
I would you were as I would have you to be.

Viola:
Would it be better, madam, than I am?
I wish it might, for now I am your fool.

Olivia:
(Aside) O what a deal of scorn looks beautiful
In the contempt and anger of his lip!
A murd'rous guilt shows not itself more soon
Than love that would seem hid. Love's night is noon. —
Cesario, by the roses of the spring,
By maidhood, honour, truth, and everything,
I love thee so, that maugre all thy pride,
Nor wit nor reason can my passion hide.
Do not extort thy reasons from this clause;
But rather reason thus with reason fetter:
Love sought is good, but given unsought is better.

Viola:
By innocence I swear, and by my youth,
I have one heart, one bosom, and one truth,
And that no woman has; nor never none
Shall mistress be of it, save I alone.
And so, adieu, good madam; never more
Will I my master's tears to you deplore.

Olivia:
Yet come again: for thou perhaps mayst move
That heart which now abhors, to like his love.

TARTUFFE ACT 2 SC 3
BY MOLIERE (1664)

(Dorine is scolding her mistress, Mariane, for her inability to stand up to her father regarding her reluctance to marry Tartuffe. Dorine reminds Mariane that she loves Valere and must do everything she can to enable her relationship with Valere to flourish).

Dorine:
Tell me, have you lost your tongue, and do I have to play your part for you? Allow someone to propose such a mad project without the lightest word of resistance!

Mariane:
What do you want me to do against a father's absolute power?

Dorine:
Tell him the heart doesn't love through someone else;
that you're not getting married for him but yourself;
that since you're the one for whom the business is done,
it's you – not him – whom the husband should please.
And that if he finds his Tartuffe so delicious,
he can marry him without any hindrance!

Mariane:
I admit a father has so much power over us that I have never had the strength to speak up for myself.

Dorine:
Let's think this out. Valere has taken steps to marry you. Do you love him, please, or do you not?

Mariane:
Ah! How great is your injustice toward my love,
Dorine! Need you ask me such a question?
Have I not a hundred times disclosed to you my heart?
And don't you know the full extent of my tender passion?

Dorine:
How do I know whether your mouth was speaking for your heart,

or if this suitor has really stirred your affection?

Mariane:
You do me great wrong, Dorine, to doubt it – my true feelings
have shone forth only too clearly.

Dorine:
In short, you do love him?

Mariane:
Yes, with an extremity of passion.

Dorine:
And, at least in appearance, he loves you the same?

Mariane:
I believe so.

Dorine:
And likewise, both of you are dying to be married to each other?

Mariane:
Certainly.

Dorine:
What do you have in mind, then, about this other match?

Mariane:
To put myself to death if I am forced.

Dorine:
Very good! That's a resource I hadn't thought of. To get out of
trouble all you have to do is die. The cure is certainly wonderful. I
get furious when I hear talk like that!

Mariane:
My goodness, Dorine, what a pet you're getting into! You don't
sympathize with people in distress.

Dorine:
I don't sympathize with people who talk twaddle and who, at the moment of decision, go limp, as you do.

Mariane:
But can I help it if I'm timid?

Dorine:
But love demands firmness of heart.

Mariane:
But haven't I been firm in my love for Valere? And isn't it up to him to obtain my father's permission?

Dorine:
But look, if your father is an absolute wild man, who is completely infatuated with his Tartuffe and calls off the match he had decided on, can you blame that on your sweetheart?

Mariane:
But, by a great refusal and signal scorn, shall I reveal a heart too smitten with its choice? Shall I put aside for him – however splendid his worth – womanly modesty and filial duty? And do you want my tender ardour displayed to all the world …?

Dorine:
No, no, I don't want a thing; I see you want to belong to Monsieur Tartuffe, and now that I think of it, I'd be wrong to turn you away from such an alliance. What reason would I have to combat your wishes? In itself it is quite a superior catch. Monsieur Tartuffe! Oh-ho! Is this just anybody being proposed? Certainly, Monsieur Tartuffe, when properly considered, is not a man – to be sneezed at, and it's no small fortune to be his better half. Already everyone crowns him with glory; He's a nobleman back home, a fine figure of a man. He has a ruddy ear and florid complexion; You'll live only too happily with such a husband.

Mariane:
My goodness …

Dorine:
What joy you will have in your heart when you see yourself the wife of so handsome a husband!

Mariane:
Oh, please stop such talk and find me some way out of this marriage. I'm done for, I give in – I'm ready to do anything.

Dorine:
No, a girl must obey her father, even if he'd give her a monkey for a husband.

Mariane:
Ah, you're making me die! Try to think of a plan to save my life. Oh, Dorine, have pity.

Dorine:
Tartuffe is your man, and you'll get a taste.

Mariane:
You know that I have always confided only in you. Please do …

Dorine:
No, you have to be tartuffed.

Mariane:
All right! Since you cannot be moved by my fate, leave me alone henceforth to my despair. From desperation my heart will find its help, And I know the infallible cure for all my ills. *(She starts to leave).*

Dorine:
Oh, there, there, now, come back. I'll stop being angry. A person has to have pity on you in spite of everything.

Mariane:
You see, if I am exposed to this cruel martyrdom, I tell you, Dorine, I shall simply expire.

<u>Dorine:</u>
Don't torment yourself – with a little skill we can prevent … But here is Valere, your sweetheart.

THE RESTORATION PERIOD 1642-1660

The restoration period refers to the time of the restoration of the British monarchy. Charles 2nd regained the throne in 1660. Prior to this period, from 1642-1660, all theatres were closed and many had fallen into disrepair. This was during the time of the civil war when Oliver Cromwell and the parliamentarians took over Britain and all theatres were closed to prevent public disorder and were to remain closed until 1660, a total of eighteen years. The Puritans disapproved of the theatre, regarding it as immoral. The theatres were not all technically closed, some were used for other functions or gatherings.

The writing which emerged during this time was highly stylised, with overly complicated plots, stock characters and bawdiness. Most of the plays were comic in nature and style as a direct result of the harsh puritanical period which preceded it. For the first time, professional actresses emerged on the English stage. The audiences were mostly delighted at the novelty of experiencing female actors on our stages, rather than boys playing women's parts. The writing of this time was referred to as 'Restoration Comedy' or 'Comedy of Manners'. Many of the actors and actresses during this period became celebrities. There were many writers of these restoration comedies. George Etherege led the way with the comedy of intrigue and was followed by William Congreve, William Wycherley and Richard Brinsley Sheridan.

William Congreve 1670-1729
Congreve was best known for his plays, "The Old Bachelor", 'Love for Love", The Double Dealer" and "The Way of the World".

Richard Brinsley Sheridan 1751-1816
Sheridan was the owner of the Theatre Royal, Drury Lane. Sheridan was best known for his plays, "The Rivals", "The School for Scandal", "The Duenna", and "A Trip to Scarborough".

THE RIVALS ACT 1 SC 2 (1775)
BY RICHARD BRINSLEY SHERIDAN

(Julia Melville pays a visit to her cousin, Lydia Languish. Julia informs her that her aunt, Mrs Malaprop, has intercepted a letter to Lydia's new lover, the low-ranking Ensign Beverley and she is to be confined to her room. Lydia is upset as she has recently quarrelled with Beverley and will be unable to make things up easily. Julia has some concerns regarding Lydia marrying a poor suitor and Lydia retaliates by teasing Julia regarding her own relationship with Faulkland).

Lydia:

My dearest Julia, how delighted am I! - (*Embrace.*) How unexpected was this happiness!

Julia:

True, Lydia — and our pleasure is the greater. — But what has been the matter? You were denied to me at first!

Lydia:

Ah, Julia, I have a thousand things to tell you! – But first inform me what has conjured you to Bath? – Is Sir Anthony here?

Julia:

He is — we are arrived within this hour - and I suppose he will be here to wait on Mrs Malaprop as soon as he is dressed.

Lydia:

Then before we are interrupted, let me impart to you some of my distress! - I know your gentle nature will sympathise with me, though your prudence may condemn me! My letters have informed you of my whole connection with Beverley; but I have lost him, Julia! My aunt has discovered our intercourse by a note she intercepted, and has confined me ever since! Yet, would you believe it? She has absolutely fallen in love with a tall Irish baronet she met one night since she has been here, at Lady Macshuffle's rout.

Julia:

You jest, Lydia!

Lydia:

No, upon my word. – She really carries on a kind of correspondence with him, under a feigned name though, till she chooses to be known to him: but it is a Delia or Celia, I assure you.

Julia:

Then, surely, she is now more indulgent to her niece.

Lydia:

Quite the contrary. Since she has discovered her own frailty, she is become more suspicious of mine. Then I must inform you of another plague! That odious Acres is to be in Bath today: so that I protest I shall be teased out of all spirits!

Julia:

Come, come, Lydia, hope for the best Sir Anthony shall use his interest with Mrs Malaprop.

Lydia:

But you have not heard the worst. Unfortunately, I had quarrelled with my poor Beverley, just before my aunt made the discovery, and I have not seen him since to make it up.

Julia:

What was his offence?

Lydia:

Nothing at all! But I don't know how it was, as often as we had been together, we had never had a quarrel, and, somehow, I was afraid he would never give me an opportunity. So, last Thursday, I wrote a letter to myself, to inform myself that Beverley was at that time paying his addresses to another woman. I signed it your friend unknown, showed it to Beverley, charged him with his falsehood, put myself in a violent passion, and vowed I'd never see him more.

Julia:

And you let him depart so, and have not seen him since?

Lydia:

'Twas the next day my aunt found the matter out. I intended only to have teased him three days and a half, and now I've lost him for ever.

Julia:

If he is as deserving and sincere as you have represented him to me, he will never give you up so. Yet, consider, Lydia, you tell me he is but an ensign, and you have thirty thousand pounds.

Lydia:

But you know I lose most of my fortune if I marry without my aunt's consent, till of age; and that is what I have determined to do, ever since I knew the penalty. Nor could I love the man who would wish to wait a day for the alternative.

Julia:

Nay, this is Caprice!

Lydia:

What, does Julia tax me with caprice? I thought her lover Faulkland had inured her to it.

Julia:

I do not love even his faults.

Lydia:

But apropos — you have sent to him, I suppose?

Julia:

Not yet, upon my word — nor has he the least idea of my being in Bath. Sir Anthony's resolution was so sudden, I could not inform him of it.

Lydia:

Well, Julia, you are your own mistress (though under the protection of Sir Anthony), yet have you, for this long year, been a slave to the caprice, the whim, the jealousy of this ungrateful Faulkland, who will ever delay assuming the right of a husband, while you suffer him to be equally imperious as a lover.

Julia:

Nay, you are wrong entirely. We were contracted before my father's death. As for his character, you wrong him too. No, Lydia, he is too proud, too noble, to be jealous. Unused to the fopperies of love, he is negligent of the little duties expected from a lover — but being unhackneyed in the passion, his affection is ardent and sincere; and not feeling why he should be loved to the degree he wishes, he still suspects that he is not loved enough. This temper, I must own, has cost me many unhappy hours; but I have learned to think myself his debtor, for those imperfections which arise from the ardour of his attachment.

Lydia:

Well, I cannot blame you for defending him. But tell me candidly, Julia, had he never saved your life, do you think you should have been attached to him as you are? — Believe me, the rude blast that overset your boat was a prosperous gale of love to him.

Julia:

Gratitude may have strengthened my attachment to Mr Faulkland, but I loved him before he had preserved me; yet surely that alone were an obligation sufficient.

Lydia:

Obligation! why a water spaniel would have done as much! — Well, I should never think of giving my heart to a man because he could swim.

THE SCHOOL FOR SCANDAL ACT 1 SC 1
BY RICHARD BRINSLEY SHERIDAN (1777)

(Lady Sneerwell has a reputation for ruining people's marriages. She has a taste for scandal as she was ruined by it herself when she was younger. She has become a malicious gossip. In this scene, she is talking to her cousin, Verjuice, who is an accomplice in spreading the gossip and has put announcements in the newspapers. The scene takes place in Lady Sneerwell's dressing room. In some editions, the character of Verjuice is deleted and played by Lady Sneerwell's servant, Snake).

Lady Sneerwell:
The paragraphs you say were all inserted:

Verjuice:
They were madam-and as I copied them myself in a feigned hand there can be no suspicion whence they came.

Lady Sneerwell:
Did you circulate the report of Lady Brittle's Intrigue with Captain Boastall?

Verjuice:
Madam by this time, Lady Brittle is the talk of half the town - and I doubt not in a week the men will toast her as a demirep.

Lady Sneerwell:
What have you done as to the insinuation as to a certain Baronet's lady and a certain cook.

Verjuice:
That is in as fine a train as your Ladyship could wish. I told the story yesterday to my own maid with directions to communicate it directly to my hairdresser that in the common course of things must reach Mrs Clackit's ears within four-and-twenty hours and then you know the business is as good as done.

———

Lady Sneerwell:
Why truly Mrs Clackit has a very pretty talent - a great deal of industry – yet - yes - been tolerably successful in her way - to my knowledge she has been the cause of breaking off six matches, of three sons being disinherited and four daughters being turned out of doors. Of three several elopements, as many close confinements - nine separate maintenances and two divorces.

Verjuice:
She certainly has talents.

Lady Sneerwell:
But her manner is gross.

Verjuice:
'Tis very true. She generally designs well, has a free tongue and a bold invention - but her colouring is too dark and her outline often extravagant - She wants that delicacy of tint- and mellowness of sneer- which distinguish your Ladyship's scandal.

Lady Sneerwell:
Ah you are partial Verjuice.

Verjuice:
Not in the least - everybody allows that Lady Sneerwell can do more with a word or a look than many can with the most laboured detail even when they happen to have a little truth on their side to support it.

Lady Sneerwell:
Yes, my dear Verjuice. I am no hypocrite to deny the satisfaction I reap from the success of my efforts. Wounded myself, in the early part of my life by the envenomed tongue of scandal I confess I have since known no pleasure equal to the reducing of others to the level of my own injured reputation

Verjuice:
Nothing can be more natural – But my dear Lady Sneerwell, there is one affair in which you have lately employed me, wherein, I confess I am at a loss to guess your motives.

Lady Sneerwell:
I conceive you mean with respect to my neighbour, Sir Peter Teazle, and his family – And has my conduct in this matter really appeared to you so mysterious?

Verjuice:
Entirely so. An old bachelor as Sir Peter was, having taken a young wife from out of the country – as Lady Teazle is - are certainly fair subjects for a little mischievous raillery – but here are two young men - to whom Sir Peter has acted as a kind of guardian since their father's death, one an avowed admirer of yours and apparently your favourite, the other attached to Maria Sir Peter's ward – and confessedly beloved by her. Now on the face of these circumstances it is utterly unaccountable to me why you should not close with the passion of a man of such character and expectations as Mr Surface – and more so why you should be so uncommonly earnest to destroy the mutual Attachment subsisting between his Brother Charles and Maria.

Lady Sneerwell:
Then at once to unravel this mystery – I must inform you that love has no share whatever in the intercourse between Mr Surface and me.

Verjuice:
No!

Lady Sneerwell:
His real attachment is to Maria or her fortune – but finding in his brother a favoured rival, he has been obliged to mask his pretensions – and profit by my assistance.

Verjuice:
Yet still I am more puzzled why you should interest yourself in his success.

Lady Sneerwell:
Heavens! How dull you are! Must I confess that Charles – that libertine, that extravagant, that bankrupt in fortune and reputation – that he it is for whom I am thus anxious and malicious and to

gain whom I would sacrifice – everything!

Verjuice:
Now indeed – your conduct appears consistent and I no longer wonder at your enmity to Maria, but how came you and Surface so confidential?

Lady Sneerwell:
For our mutual interest – but I have found out him a long time since, although he has contrived to deceive everybody beside – I know him to be artful selfish and malicious – while with Sir Peter and indeed with all his acquaintance, he passes for a youthful miracle of prudence – good sense and benevolence.

Verjuice:
Yes, yes – I know Sir Peter vows he has not his equal in England; and, above all, he praises him as a man of sentiment.

Lady Sneerwell:
True and with the assistance of his sentiments and hypocrisy he has brought Sir Peter entirely in his interests with respect to Maria and is now I believe attempting to flatter Lady Teazle into the same good opinion towards him – while poor Charles has no friend in the house – though I fear he has a powerful one in Maria's heart, against whom we must direct our schemes.

THE WAY OF THE WORLD ACT 2
BY WILLIAM CONGREVE (1700)

(Mrs Fainall and Mrs Marwood are taking a walk in St James Park).

<u>Mrs Fainall:</u>

Ay, ay, dear Marwood, if we will be happy, we must find the means in ourselves, and among ourselves. Men are ever in extremes; either doting or averse. While they are lovers, if they have fire and sense, their jealousies are unsupportable: and when they cease to love (we ought to think at least) they loathe, they look upon us with sorrow and distaste, they meet us like the ghosts of what we were, and as from such, fly from us.

<u>Mrs Marwood:</u>

True, 'tis an unhappy circumstance of life that love should ever die before us, and that the man so often should outlive the lover. But say what you will, 'tis better to be left than never to have been loved.To pass our youth in dull indifference, to refuse the sweets of life because they once must leave us, is as preposterous as to wish to have been born old, because we one day must be old. For my part, my youth may wear and waste, but it shall never rust in my possession.

<u>Mrs Fainall:</u>
Then it seems you dissemble an aversion to mankind only in compliance to my mother's humour.

<u>Mrs Marwood:</u>

Certainly. To be free, I have no taste of those insipid dry discourses with which our sex of force must entertain themselves apart from men. We may affect endearments to each other, profess eternal friendships, and seem to dote like lovers; but 'tis not in our natures long to persevere. Love will resume his empire in our breasts, and every heart, or soon or late, receive and re-admit him as its lawful tyrant.

Mrs Fainall:
Bless me, how have I been deceived! Why, you profess a libertine.

Mrs Marwood:

You see my friendship by my freedom. Come, be sincere, acknowledge that your sentiments agree with mine.

Mrs Fainall:

Never.

Mrs Marwood:

You hate mankind?

Mrs Fainall:
Heartily, inveterately.

Mrs Marwood:

Your husband?

Mrs Fainall:
Most transcendently; ay, though I say it, meritoriously.

Mrs Marwood:
Give me your hand upon it.

Mrs Fainall:

There.

Mrs Marwood:
I join with you; what I have said has been to try you.

Mrs Fainall:
Is it possible? Dost thou hate those vipers, men?

Mrs Marwood:

I have done hating 'em, and am now come to despise 'em; the next thing I have to do is eternally to forget 'em.

Mrs Fainall:
There spoke the spirit of an Amazon.

Mrs Marwood:

And yet I am thinking sometimes to carry my aversion further.

Mrs Fainall:

How?

Mrs Marwood:

Faith, by marrying; if I could but find one that love me very well, and would be thoroughly sensible of ill-usage, I think I should do myself the violence of undergoing the ceremony.

Mrs Fainall:
You would not make him a cuckold?

Mrs Marwood:
No; but I'd make him believe I did, and that's as bad.

Mrs Fainall:
Why had not you as good do it?

Mrs Marwood:

Oh, if he should ever discover it, he would then know the worse, and be out of his pain; but I would have him ever to continue upon the rack of fear and jealousy.

—

Mrs Fainall:
Ingenious mischief! Would thou were married.

Mrs Marwood:

Would I were!

Mrs Fainall:
You change colour.

Mrs Marwood:

Because I hate him.

Mrs Fainall:

So do I; but I can hear him named. But what reason have you to hate him in particular?

Mrs Marwood:
I ever loved him; he is, and always was, insufferably proud.

Mrs Fainall:

By the reason you give for your aversion, one would think it dissembled; for you have laid a fault to his charge, of which enemies must acquit him.

Mrs Marwood:

Oh, then it seems you are one of his favourable enemies. Methinks you look a little pale, and now you flush again.

Mrs Fainall:
Do I? I think I am a little sick o' the sudden.

Mrs Marwood:

What ails you?

<u>Mrs Fainall:</u>

(She sees her husband). My husband. Don't you see him? He turned short upon me unawares, and has almost overcome me.

THE WAY OF THE WORLD ACT 3 SC 1
BY WILLIAM CONGREVE

(A play of greed, love and deceit. The aristocratic Lady Wishfort is in her dressing room when Foible enters, a servant who works for Lady Wishfort and also undercover for Mirabel. She has delivered Lady Wishfort's portrait to her new suitor, Sir Rowland. Lady Wishfort is not aware that Sir Rowland is in fact Foible's husband, a servant named Waitwell. The plan is to humiliate Lady Wishfort as she would be committing bigamy as Sir Rowland aka Waitwell is already married).

Lady Wishfort:

O Foible, where hast thou been? What hast thou been doing?

Foible:

Madam, I have seen the party.

Lady Wishfort:

But what hast thou done?

Foible:

Nay, 'tis your ladyship has done, and are to do; I have only promised. But a man so enamoured—so transported! Well, if worshipping of pictures be a sin—poor Sir Rowland, I say.

Lady Wishfort:

The miniature has been counted like. But hast thou not betrayed me, Foible? Hast thou not detected me to that faithless Mirabell? What hast thou to do with him in the park? Answer me, has he got nothing out of thee?

Foible:

So, the devil has been beforehand with me; what shall I say? Alas, madam, could I help it, if I met that confident thing? Was I in fault? If you had heard how he used me, and all upon your ladyship's account, I'm sure you would not suspect my fidelity. Nay, if that had been the worst I could have borne: but he had a fling at your ladyship too, and then I could not hold; but, i'faith I gave him his own.

Lady Wishfort:

Me? What did the filthy fellow say?

Foible:

O madam, 'tis a shame to say what he said, with his taunts and his fleers, tossing up his nose. 'Humh', says he, 'what, you are a-hatching some plot', says he, 'you are so early abroad, or catering', says he, 'ferreting for some disbanded officer, I warrant. Half pay is but thin subsistence', says he. 'Well, what pension does your lady propose? Let me see, says he, what, she must come down pretty deep now, she's superannuated, says he, and—'

Lady Wishfort:

Ods my life, I'll have him—I'll have him murdered. I'll have him poisoned. Where does he eat? I'll marry a drawer to have him poisoned in his wine. I'll send for Robin from Locket's— immediately.

Foible:

Poison him? Poisoning's too good for him. Starve him, madam, starve him; marry Sir Rowland, and get him disinherited. Oh, you would bless yourself to hear what he said.

Lady Wishfort:

A villain; superannuated?

Foible:

'Humh', says he, 'I hear you are laying designs against me too', says he, 'and Mrs. Millamant is to marry my uncle' (he does not suspect a word of your ladyship); 'but," says he, I'll fit you for that, I warrant you", says he, I'll hamper you for that, says he, 'you and your old frippery too', says he, 'I'll handle you—'

Lady Wishfort:

Audacious villain! Handle me? Would he durst? Frippery? Old frippery? Was there ever such a foul-mouthed fellow? I'll be married to-morrow, I'll be contracted to-night.

Foible:

The sooner the better, madam.

Lady Wishfort:

Will Sir Rowland be here, say'st thou? When, Foible?

Foible:

Incontinently, madam. No new sheriff's wife expects the return of her husband after knighthood with that impatience in which Sir Rowland burns for the dear hour of kissing your ladyship's hand after dinner.

Lady Wishfort:

Frippery? Superannuated frippery? I'll frippery the villain; I'll reduce him to frippery and rags, a tatterdemalion!—I hope to see him hung with tatters, like a Long Lane pent-house, or a gibbet thief. A slander-mouthed railer! I warrant the spendthrift prodigal's in debt as much as the million lottery, or the whole court upon a birthday. I'll spoil his credit with his tailor. Yes, he shall have my niece with her fortune, he shall.

Foible:

He? I hope to see him lodge in Ludgate first, and angle into Blackfriars for brass farthings with an old mitten.

Lady Wishfort:

Ay, dear Foible; thank thee for that, dear Foible. He has put me out of all patience. I shall never recompose my features to receive Sir Rowland with any economy of face. This wretch has fretted me that I am absolutely decayed. Look, Foible.

Foible: (referring to Lady Wishfort's cracking make-up).

Your ladyship has frowned a little too rashly, indeed, madam. There are some cracks discernible in the white vernish.

Lady Wishfort:

Let me see the glass. Cracks, say'st thou? Why, I am arrantly flayed: I look like an old peeled wall. Thou must repair me, Foible, before Sir Rowland comes, or I shall never keep up to my picture.

Foible:

I warrant you, madam: a little art once made your picture like you, and now a little of the same art must make you like your picture. Your picture must sit for you, madam.

Lady Wishfort:

But art thou sure Sir Rowland will not fail to come? Or will a not fail when he does come? Will he be importunate, Foible, and push? For if he should not be importunate I shall never break decorums. I shall die with confusion if I am forced to advance—oh no, I can never advance; I shall swoon if he should expect advances. No, I hope Sir Rowland is better bred than to put a lady to the necessity of breaking her forms. I won't be too coy neither— I won't give him despair. But a little disdain is not amiss; a little scorn is alluring.

Foible:

A little scorn becomes your ladyship.

Lady Wishfort:

Yes, but tenderness becomes me best—a sort of a dyingness. You see that picture has a sort of a—ha, Foible? A swimmingness in the eyes. Yes, I'll look so. My niece affects it; but she wants features. Is Sir Rowland handsome? Let my toilet be removed—I'll dress above. I'll receive Sir Rowland here. Is he handsome? Don't answer me. I won't know; I'll be surprised. I'll be taken by surprise.

—

Foible:

By storm, madam. Sir Rowland's a brisk man.

Lady Wishfort:

Is he? Oh, then, he'll importune, if he's a brisk man. I shall save decorums if Sir Rowland importunes. I have a mortal terror at the apprehension of offending against decorums. Oh, I'm glad he's a brisk man. Let my things be removed, good Foible.

LOUISA MAY ALCOTT 1832-1888

Louisa May Alcott was an American writer best known for the novel 'Little Women'. The story follows the March family of four daughters, Meg, Jo, Amy and Beth. The sequels were 'Little Men' and 'Jo's Boys' and all follow the lives of the March family and covers the period of the American Civil War. The story is semi biographical. Alcott wrote the novel of Little Women to help her father. She wanted to write a novel about girls and so she wrote the story of her adolescence growing up with her three sisters. Louisa also wrote any short stories and poems. Louisa never married, preferring to devote her time to her career. During her lifetime, Louisa worked as a Civil War nurse as well as fighting against slavery. She also registered women to vote. Louisa's family home is now open to the public and is designated as a National Historic Landmark.

LITTLE WOMEN BY LOUISA MAY ALCOTT (1868)

(The two March girls have been invited to a dance on New Year's Eve at Mrs Gardiner's).

Meg:

Jo! Jo! Where are you?

Jo:

Here!

Meg:

Such fun! Only see! A regular note of invitation from Mrs. Gardiner for tomorrow night! 'Mrs. Gardiner would be happy to see Miss March and Miss Josephine at a little dance on New Year's Eve.' Marmee is willing we should go, now what shall we wear?

Jo:

What's the use of asking that, when you know we shall wear our poplins, because we haven't got anything else?

Meg:

If I only had a silk! Mother says I may when I'm eighteen perhaps, but two years is an everlasting time to wait.

Jo:

I'm sure our pops look like silk, and they are nice enough for us. Yours is as good as new, but I forgot the burn and the tear in mine. Whatever shall I do? The burn shows badly, and I can't take it out.

Meg:

You must sit still all you can and keep your back out of sight. The front is all right. I shall have a new ribbon for my hair, and Marmee will lend me her little pearl pin, and my new slippers are lovely, and my gloves will do, though they aren't as nice as I'd like.

Jo:

Mine are spoiled with lemonade, and I can't get any new ones, so I shall have to go without. I never trouble myself much about dress.

Meg:

You must have gloves, or I won't go. Gloves are more important than anything else. You can't dance without them, and if you don't, I should be so mortified.

Jo:

Then I'll stay still. I don't care much for company dancing. It's no fun to go sailing round. I like to fly about and cut capers.

Meg:

You can't ask Mother for new ones, they are so expensive, and you are so careless. She said when you spoiled the others that she shouldn't get you anymore this winter. Can't you make them do?

Jo:

I can hold them crumpled up in my hand, so no one will know how stained they are. That's all I can do. No! I'll tell you how we can manage, each wear one good one and carry a bad one. Don't you see?

Meg:

Your hands are bigger than mine, and you will stretch my glove dreadfully.

Jo:

Then I'll go without. I don't care what people say!

Meg:

You may have it, you may! Only don't stain it, and do behave nicely. Don't put your hands behind you, or stare, or say 'Christopher Columbus!' will you?

<u>Jo:</u>

Don't worry about me. I'll be as prim as I can and not get into any scrapes, if I can help it. Now go and answer your note, and let me finish this splendid story.

OSCAR WILDE 1854-1900

Oscar Wilde was born in Dublin, Ireland. He was the son of an ear and eye surgeon and a writer and poet mother, Jane Francesca Elgee. He won the top prize for Classics at school and was later educated at Trinity College, Dublin. He then went on to study at Magdalen College, Oxford. From Oxford, Wilde moved to London to pursue a literary career. Wilde's literary work was prolific and during his career he moved to New York for nine months and delivered 140 lectures.

Oscar married Constance Lloyd in 1884. The couple had two sons together, Cyril and Vyvyan. Later, Constance moved to Switzerland with their two children in an attempt to avoid the scandal of her husband's notorious affair.

In 1891, he pursued an affair with Lord Alfred Douglas, whose nickname was Bosie. Unfortunately, this affair became rather public as Bosie was the son of the Marquis of Queensberry. Lord Queensberry was outraged by the public nature of this illegal relationship. In1895 Oscar Wilde sued Douglas's father, the Marquis of Queensberry, for libel over accusations of homosexuality. Wilde lost the case and was arrested and imprisoned for 2 years. He was firstly incarcerated at Newgate prison, then at Pentonville prison and was then transferred to Wandsworth prison, eventually ending his sentence in Reading Gaol. He was spat at and jeered at on his transferral to Reading Prison. The conditions were grim. At first, he was not even allowed writing materials but at a later date was granted these privileges. On release from prison, Wilde immediately went into exile to France. He never returned to England. In 1900, he died of meningitis in Paris aged 46yrs and was buried there. Wilde received a posthumous pardon in 2017 when homosexuality was thankfully no longer considered a crime.

He was deeply committed to **aestheticism** throughout his life. Oscar Wilde's writing style is unique. He writes with a mixture of realism and fantasy. His observation of character and social status puts him among the best of writers. His wit, intellect and use of satire is highly amusing, decadent as well as extremely critical.

His plays are considered 'comedy of manners' and provide a satirical portrayal of behaviour amongst the upper echelons of Victorian society. His portrayal of wealth, snobbery and morality are insurmountable. He satirises the repression of the upper classes of Victorian Britain and examines the morality and philosophy of the period.

LADY WINDERMERE'S FAN ACT 1
BY OSCAR WILDE (1892)

(The Duchess of Berwick addresses Lady Windermere. She is very keen to point out the effect of Mrs Erlynne's arrival and subsequent impact on society).

Duchess of Berwick:
And now I must tell you how sorry I am for you, dear Margaret. (*she crosses and sits next to her*)

Lady Windermere:
Why, Duchess?

Duchess of Berwick:
Oh, on account of that horrid woman. She dresses so well, too, which makes it much worse, sets such a dreadful example. Augustus – you know my disreputable brother – such a trial to us all – well, Augustus is completely infatuated about her. It is quite scandalous, for she is absolutely inadmissible into society. Many a woman has a past, but I am told that she has at least a dozen, and they all fit.

Lady Windermere:
Whom are you talking about, Duchess?

Duchess of Berwick:
About Mrs Erlynne?

Lady Windermere:
I never heard of her, Duchess. And what has she to do with me?

Duchess of Berwick:
My poor child!

Lady Windermere:
Why do you talk to me about this person?

Duchess of Berwick:
Don't you really know? I assure you we're all so distressed about it. Only last night at dear Lady Jansen's everyone was saying how extraordinary it was that, of all men in London, Windermere should behave in such a way

Lady Windermere:
My husband - what has he got to do with any woman of that kind?

Duchess of Berwick:
Ah, what indeed, dear? That is the point. He goes to see her continually, and stops for hours at a time, and while he is there, she is not at home to anyone. Not that many ladies call on her, dear, but she has a great many disreputable men friends – my own brother particularly, as I told you – and that is what makes it so dreadful about Windermere. We looked upon *him* as being such a model husband, but I am afraid there is no doubt about it. My dear nieces – you know the Saville girls, don't you? – such nice domestic creatures – dreadfully plain. This terrible woman has taken a house in Curzon Street, right opposite them – such a respectable street, too! I don't know what we're coming to! And they tell me that Windermere goes there four or five times a week – they *see* him. And the worst of it all is that I have been told that this woman has got a great deal of money out of somebody, for it seems that she came to London six months ago without anything at all to speak of, and now she has this charming house in Mayfair, drives her ponies in the Park every afternoon and all – well, all – since she has known poor dear Windermere.

Lady Windermere:
Oh, I can't believe it!

Duchess of Berwick:

But it's quite true, my dear. The whole of London knows it. That is why I felt it was better to come and talk to you, and advise you to take Windermere away at once to Hamburg or to Aix, where he'll have something to amuse him, and where you can watch him all day long. I assure you, my dear, that on several occasions after I was first married, I had to pretend to be very ill, merely to get Berwick out of town. He was so extremely susceptible. Though I am bound to say he never gave away any large sums of money to anybody. He is far too high-principled for that!

Lady Windermere:

Duchess, Duchess, it's impossible! We are only married two years. Our child is but six months old.

Duchess of Berwick:

How is the little darling? Is it a boy or a girl? Ah, I remember it's a boy! I'm so sorry. Boys are so wicked. My boy is excessively immoral. You wouldn't believe at what hours he comes home. And he's only left Oxford a few months – I really don't know what they teach them there.

Lady Windermere:

Are all men bad?

Duchess of Berwick:

Oh, all of them, my dear, all of them, without any exception. And they never grow any better. Men become old, but they never become good.

Lady Windermere:

Windermere and I married for love.

Duchess of Berwick:

Yes, we begin like that. It was only Berwick's brutal and incessant threats of suicide that made me accept him at all and before the year was out, he was running after all kinds of petticoats. In fact, before the honeymoon was over, I caught him winking at my maid, a most pretty, respectable girl. I dismissed her at once without a character. No, I remember I passed her on to my sister; poor dear Sir George is so short-sighted, I thought it wouldn't matter. But it did, though – it was most unfortunate. And mind you don't take this little aberration of Windermere's too much to heart. Just take him abroad, and he'll come back to you all right.

LADY WINDERMERE'S FAN ACT 3
BY OSCAR WILDE (1892)

(In Lord Darlington's rooms. Mrs Erlynne pays a visit to Lady Windermere).

Mrs Erlynne:
Lady Windermere! (*Lady Windermere is startled*). Thank Heaven I am in time. You must go back to your husband's house immediately.

Lady Windermere:
Must?

Mrs Erlynne:
Yes, you must! There is not a second to be lost. Lord Darlington may return at any moment.

Lady Windermere:
Don't come near me!

Mrs Erlynne:
Oh! You are on the brink of ruin, you are on the brink of a hideous precipice. You must leave this place at once; my carriage is waiting at the corner of the street. You must come with me and drive straight home. *(Lady Windermere throws off her cloak & flings it on the sofa)* What are you doing?

Lady Windermere:
Mrs Erlynne – if you had not come here, I would have gone back. But now that I see you, I feel that nothing in the whole world would induce me to live under the same roof as Lord Windermere. There is something about you that stirs the wildest- rage within me. And I know why you are here. My husband sent you to lure me back that I might serve as a blind to whatever relations exist between you

and him.

Mrs Erlynne:
Oh! You don't think that – you can't.

Lady Windermere:
Go back to my husband, Mrs Erlynne. He belongs to you and not to me. I suppose he is afraid of a scandal. Men are such cowards. They outrage every law of the world, and are afraid of the world's tongue. But he had better prepare himself. He shall have a scandal. He shall have the worst scandal there has been in London for years. He shall see his name in every vile paper, mine on every hideous placard.

Mrs Erlynne:
No – no –

Lady Windermere:
Yes! He shall. Had he come himself, I admit I would have gone back to the life of degradation you and he had prepared for me - but to stay himself at home, and to send you as his messenger – oh! It was infamous.

Mrs Erlynne:
Lady Windermere, you wrong me horribly – you wrong your husband horribly. He doesn't know you are here. He never read the mad letter you wrote to him!

Lady Windermere:
Never read it!

Mrs Erlynne:
No – he knows nothing about it.

Lady Windermere:
How simple you think me! You are lying to me!

Mrs Erlynne:
I am not. I am telling the truth.

Lady Windermere:
If my husband didn't read the letter, how is it that you are here? Who told you I had left the house you were shameless enough to enter: who told you where I had gone? My husband told you, and sent you to decoy me back.

Mrs Erlynne:
Your husband has never seen the letter. I - saw it, I opened it. I - read it.

Lady Windermere:
You opened a letter of mine to my husband? You wouldn't dare!

Mrs Erlynne:
To save you from the abyss into which you are falling, there is nothing in the world I would not dare. Here is the letter. Your husband has never read it. He never shall read it. It should never have been written.

(*She tears it up and throws it into the fire*)

Lady Windermere:
How do I know that that was my letter after all? You seem to think that commonest device can take me in!

Mrs Erlynne:
Oh! Why do you disbelieve everything I tell you? What object do you think I have in coming here, except to save you from utter ruin, to save you from the consequence of a hideous mistake?

That letter that is burnt now was *your* letter. I swear it to you!

Lady Windermere:
You took good care to burn it before I had examined it. I cannot trust you. You, whose whole life is a lie, how could you speak the truth about anything?

Mrs Erlynne:
Think as you like about me – say what you choose against me, but go back, go back to the husband you love.

Lady Windermere:
I do not love him!

Mrs Erlynne:
You do, and you know that he loves you.

Lady Windermere:
He does not understand what love is. He understands it as little as you do – but I see what you want. It would be a great advantage for you to get me back. Dear Heaven! What a life I would have then! Living at the mercy of a woman who comes between husband and wife!

Mrs Erlynne:
Lady Windermere, Lady Windermere, don't say such terrible things. You don't know how terrible they are, how terrible and how unjust. Listen, you must listen! Only go back to your husband, and I promise you never to communicate with him again on any pretext – never to see him - never to have anything to do with his life or yours. The money that he gave me, he gave me not through love, but through hatred. The hold I have over him –

Lady Windermere:
Ah! You admit you have a hold!

Mrs Erlynne:
Yes, and I will tell you what it is. It is his love for you, Lady
Windermere.

Lady Windermere:
You expect me to believe that?

Mrs Erlynne:
You must believe it! It is true. It is his love for you that has made
him submit to – oh! Call it what you like, tyranny, threats, anything
you choose. But it is his love for you. His desire to spare you –
shame and disgrace.

Lady Windermere:
What do you mean? You are insolent! What have I to do with you?

Mrs Erlynne:
Nothing. I know it – but I tell you that your husband loves you –
that you may never meet with such love again in your whole life –
and that if you throw it away, the day may come when you will
starve for love and it will not be given to you. Arthur loves you!

Lady Windermere:
Arthur? And you tell me there is nothing between you?

Mrs Erlynne:
Lady Windermere, before Heaven your husband is guiltless of all
offence towards you! And I – I tell you that if, had it ever occurred
to me, that such a monstrous suspicion would have entered your
mind, I would have died rather than have crossed your life or his!

Lady Windermere:
You talk as if you had a heart. Women like you have no hearts.

Mrs Erlynne:

Believe what you choose about me. But don't spoil your beautiful young life on my account! You don't know what may be in store for you, unless you leave this house at once. You don't know what it is to find the door shut against one. One pays for one's sin, and then one pays again, and all one's life one pays. You must never know that. I may have wrecked my own life, but I will not let you wreck yours! No! Go back, Lady Windermere, to the husband who loves you, whom you love. You have a child, Lady Windermere. Go back to that child. Back to your house, Lady Windermere – your husband loves you! He has never swerved for a moment from the love he bears you. You must stay with your child.

(Lady Windermere burst into tears)

Lady Windermere:
Take me home.

Mrs Erlynne:
Come! Where is your cloak? Put it on. Come at once.

Lady Windermere:
Stop! Don't you hear voices? That is my husband's voice! He is coming in! Save me! Oh, it's some plot! You have sent for him.

Mrs Erlynne:
Silence! I'm here to save you, if I can.

THE IMPORTANCE OF BEING EARNEST ACT 2 (1894)

(Cecily Cardew and Miss Prism, her tutor, are in the garden at the Manor House. It is July. Basket chairs and a table covered with books are set under a large yew tree. Cecily is watering flowers).

Miss Prism:
Cecily, Cecily! Surely such a utilitarian occupation as the watering of flowers is rather Moulton's duty than yours? Especially at a moment when intellectual pleasures await you. Your German grammar is on the table. Pray open it at page fifteen. We will repeat yesterday's lesson.

Cecily:
But I don't like German. It isn't at all a becoming language. I know perfectly well that I look quite plain after my German lesson.

Miss Prism:
Child, you know how anxious your guardian is that you should improve yourself in every way. He laid particular stress on your German, as he was leaving for town yesterday. Indeed, he always lays stress on your German when he is leaving for town.

Cecily:
Dear Uncle Jack is so very serious! Sometimes he is so serious that I think he cannot be quite well.

Miss Prism:
Your guardian enjoys the best of health, and his gravity of demeanour is especially to be commended in one so comparatively young as his is. I know no one who has a higher sense of duty and responsibility.

Cecily:
I suppose that is why he often looks a little bored when we three are together.

Miss Prism:
Cecily! I am surprised at you. Mr Worthing has many troubles in his life. Idle merriment and triviality would be out of place in his conversation. You must remember his constant anxiety about that unfortunate young man, his brother.

Cecily:
I wish Uncle Jack would allow that unfortunate young man, his brother, to come down here sometimes. We might have a good influence over him, Miss Prism. I am sure you certainly would. You know German, and geology, and things of that kind influence a man very much. *(Cecily begins to write in her diary).*

Miss Prism:
I do not think that even I could produce any effect on a character that according to his own brother's admission is irretrievably weak and vacillating. Indeed, I am not sure that I would desire to reclaim him. I am not in favour of this modern mania for turning bad people into good people at a moment's notice. As a man sows so let him reap. You must put away your diary, Cecily. I really don't see why you should keep a diary at all.

Cecily:
I keep a diary in order to enter the wonderful secrets of my life. If I didn't write them down, I should probably forget all about them.

Miss Prism:
Memory, my dear Cecily, is the diary that we all carry about with us.

Cecily:

Yes, but it usually chronicles the things that have never happened, and couldn't possibly have happened. I believe that Memory is responsible for nearly all the three-volume novels that Mudie sends us.

Miss Prism:

Do not speak slightingly of the three-volume novel, Cecily. I wrote one myself in earlier days.

Cecily:

Did you really, Miss Prism? How wonderfully clever you are! I hope it did not end happily? I don't like novels that end happily. They depress me so much.

Miss Prism:

The good ended happily, and the bad unhappily. That is what Fiction means.

Cecily:

I suppose so. But it seems very unfair. And was your novel ever published?

Miss Prism:

Alas! No. The manuscript unfortunately was abandoned. I use the word in the sense of lost or mislaid. To your work, child, these speculations are profitless.

THE IMPORTANCE OF BEING EARNEST ACT 2
BY OSCAR WILDE (1894)

(Cecily Cardew is visited by Gwendolen Fairfax in the garden of Jack's country estate).

Cecily:
Pray let me introduce myself to you. My Name is Cecily Cardew.

Gwendolen:
Cecily Cardew? What a very sweet name! Something tells me that we are going to be great friends. I like you already more than I can say. My first impressions of people are never wrong.

Cecily:
How nice of you to like me so much after we have known each other such a comparatively short time. Pray sit down.

Gwendolen: *(still standing up)*
I may call you Cecily, may I not?

Cecily:
With pleasure!

Gwendolen:
And you will always call me Gwendolen, won't you?

Cecily:
If you wish.

Gwendolen:
Then that is all quite settled, is it not?

Cecily:
I hope so. (*They both sit down together*)

Gwendolen:
Perhaps this might be a favourable opportunity for my mentioning who I am. My father is Lord Bracknell. You have never heard of Papa, I suppose?

Cecily:
I don't think so.

Gwendolen:
Outside the family circle, Papa, I am glad to say, is entirely unknown. I think that is quite as it should be. The home seems to me to be the proper sphere for the man. And certainly, once a man begins to neglect his domestic duties, he becomes painfully effeminate, does he not? And I don't like that. It makes men so very attractive. Cecily, Mamma, whose views on education are remarkably strict, has brought me up to be extremely short-sighted; it is part of her system; so, do you mind my looking at you through my glasses?

Cecily:
Oh! not at all, Gwendolen. I am very fond of being looked at.

Gwendolen: (*She examines Cecily through a lorgnette*)
You are here on a short visit, I suppose.

Cecily:
Oh no! I live here.

Gwendolen:
Really? Your mother, no doubt, or some female relative of advanced years, resides here also?

Cecily:
Oh no! I have no mother, nor, in fact, any relations.

Gwendolen:
Indeed?

Cecily:
My dear guardian, with the assistance of Miss Prism, has the arduous task of looking after me.

Gwendolen:
Your guardian?

Cecily:
Yes, I am Mr Worthing's ward.

Gwendolen:
Oh! It is strange he never mentioned to me that he had a ward. How secretive of him! He grows more interesting hourly. I am not sure, however, that the news inspires me with feelings of unmixed delight. I am very fond of you, Cecily; I have liked you ever since I met you! But I am bound to state that now that I know that you are Mr Worthing's ward, I cannot help expressing a wish you were – well, just a little older than you seem to be – and not quite so very alluring in appearance. In fact, if I may speak candidly –

Cecily:
Pray do! I think that whenever one has anything unpleasant to say, one should always be quite candid.

Gwendolen:
Well, to speak with perfect candour, Cecily, I wish you were fully forty-two, and more than usually plain for your age. Ernest has a strong upright nature. He is the very soul of truth and honour. Disloyalty would be as impossible to him as deception. But even men of the noblest possible moral character are extremely susceptible to the influence of the physical charms of others. Modern, no less that Ancient History, supplies us with many most

painful examples of what I refer to. If it were not so, indeed, History would be quite unreadable.

Cecily:
I beg your pardon, Gwendolen, did you say Ernest?

Gwendolen:
Yes.

Cecily:
Oh, but it is not Mr Ernest Worthing who is my guardian. It is his brother – his elder brother.

Gwendolen:
Ernest never mentioned to me that he had a brother.

Cecily:
I am sorry to say they have not been on good terms for a long time.

Gwendolen:
Ah! That accounts for it. And now that I think of it, I have never heard any man mention his brother. The subject seems distasteful to most men. Cecily, you have lifted a load from my mind. I was growing almost anxious. It would have been terrible if any cloud had come across a friendship like ours, would it not? Of course, you are quite, quite sure that it is not Mr Ernest Worthing who is your guardian?

Cecily:
Quite sure. (*Pause*) In fact, I am going to be his.

Gwendolen:
I beg your pardon?

<u>Cecily:</u> (*confidingly*)
Dearest Gwendolen, there is no reason why I should make a secret of it to you. Our little county newspaper is sure to chronicle the fact next week. Mr Ernest Worthing and I are engaged to be married.

<u>Gwendolen:</u> (*rising*)
My darling Cecily, I think there must be some slight error. Mr Ernest Worthing is engaged to me. The announcement will appear in the *Morning Post* on Saturday at the latest.

<u>Cecily:</u> (*rising*)
I am afraid you must be under some misconception. Ernest proposed to me exactly ten minutes ago. (*She shows her diary*)

<u>Gwendolen:</u>
It is very curious, for he asked me to be his wife yesterday afternoon at 5.30. If you would care to verify the incident, pray do so. (*She produces her own diary*). I never travel without my diary. One should always have something sensational to read in the train. I am so sorry, dear Cecily, if it is any disappointment to you, but I am afraid I have the prior claim.

<u>Cecily:</u>
It would distress me more that I can tell you, dear Gwendolen, if it has caused you any mental or physical anguish, but I feel bound to point out that since Ernest proposed to you. he clearly has changed his mind.

<u>Gwendolen:</u>
If the poor fellow has been entrapped into any foolish promise, I shall consider it my duty to rescue him at once, and with a firm hand.

Cecily:
Whatever unfortunate entanglement my dear boy may have gotten into, I will never reproach him with it after we are married.

Gwendolen:
Do you allude to me, Miss Cardew, as an entanglement? You are presumptuous. On an occasion of this kind, it becomes more than a moral duty to speak one's mind. It becomes a pleasure.

Cecily:
Do you suggest, Miss Fairfax, that I entrapped Ernest into an engagement? How dare you? This is no time for wearing the shallow mask of manners. When I see a spade, I call it a spade.

Gwendolen:
I am glad to say that I have never seen a spade. It is obvious that our social spheres have been widely different. *(A pause whilst Merriman brings in the tea on a silver salver)* Are there many interesting walks in the vicinity, Miss Cardew?

Cecily:
Oh! Yes! A great many. From the top of one of the hills quite close one can see five counties.

Gwendolen:
Five counties! I don't think I should like that; I hate crowds.

Cecily:
I suppose that is why you live in town?

Gwendolen:
Quite a well-kept garden this is, Miss Cardew.

Cecily:
So glad you like it, Miss Fairfax.

Gwendolen:
I had no idea there were any flowers in the country.

Cecily:
Oh, flowers are as common here, Miss Fairfax, as people are in London.

Gwendolen:
Personally, I cannot understand how anybody manages to exist in the country, if anybody who is anybody does. The country always bores me to death.

Cecily:
Ah! This is what the newspapers call agricultural depression, is it not? I believe the aristocracy are suffering very much from it just at present. It is almost an epidemic amongst them, I have been told. May I offer you some tea, Miss Fairfax?

Gwendolen:
Thank you. (*Aside*). Detestable girl! But I require tea!

Cecily:
Sugar?

Gwendolen:
No, thank you. Sugar is not fashionable anymore. (*Cecily takes the tongs and puts four lumps of sugar into the cup*).

Cecily:
Cake or bread and butter?

Gwendolen:
Bread and butter, please. Cake is rarely seen at the best houses nowadays. *(She tastes the tea)*. You have filled my tea with lumps of sugar, and though I asked most distinctly for bread and butter,

you have given me cake. I am known for the gentleness of my disposition, and the extraordinary sweetness of my nature, but I warn you, Miss Cardew, you may go too far.

Cecily:
To save my poor, innocent, trusting boy from the machinations of any other girl there are no lengths to which I would not go.

Gwendolen:
From the moment I saw you I distrusted you. I felt that you were false and deceitful. I am never deceived in such matters. My first impressions of people are invariably right.

Cecily:
It seems to me, Miss Fairfax, that I am trespassing on your valuable time. No doubt you have many other calls of a similar character to make in the neighbourhood.

AN IDEAL HUSBAND ACT 2
BY OSCAR WILDE (1893)

(Mrs Cheveley is visiting Gertrude Chiltern's home. Lady Markby has just left and the two women share a moment alone. There is no love lost between the two women. Sir Robert Chiltern enters towards the end of the scene).

Mrs Cheveley:
Wonderful woman, Lady Markby, isn't she? Talks more and says less than anybody I ever met. She is made to be a public speaker. Much more so than her husband, though he is a typical Englishman, always dull and usually violent.

Lady Chiltern:
Mrs Cheveley, I think it is right to tell you quite frankly that, had I known who you really were, I should not have invited you to my house last night.

Mrs Cheveley: (*with an impertinent smile*)
Really?

Lady Chiltern:
I could not have done so.

Mrs Cheveley:
I see that after all these years you have not changed a bit, Gertrude.

Lady Chiltern:
I never change.

Mrs Cheveley:
Then life has taught you nothing?

Lady Chiltern:
It has taught me that a person who has once been guilty of a dishonest and dishonourable action may be guilty of it a second time, and should be shunned.

Mrs Cheveley:
Would you apply that rule to everyone?

Lady Chiltern:
Yes, to everyone, without exception.

Mrs Cheveley:
Then I am sorry for you, Gertrude, very sorry for you.

Lady Chiltern:
You see now, I am sure, that for many reasons any further acquaintance between us during your stay in London is quite impossible?

Mrs Cheveley:
Do you know, Gertrude, I don't mind your talking morality a bit. Morality is simply the attitude we adopt towards people who we personally dislike. You dislike me. I am quite aware of that. And I have always detested you. And yet I have come here to do you a service.

Lady Chiltern:
Like the service you wished to render my husband last night, I suppose. Thank heaven, I saved him from that.

Mrs Cheveley:
It was you made him write that insolent letter to me? It was you who made him break his promise?

Lady Chiltern:
Yes.

Mrs Cheveley:
Then you must make him keep it. I give you till tomorrow morning
– no more. If by the time your husband does not solemnly bind
himself to help me in this great scheme in which I am interested –

Lady Chiltern:
This fraudulent speculation –

Mrs Cheveley:
Call it what you choose. I hold your husband in the hollow of my
hand, and if you are wise, you will make him do what I tell him.

Lady Chiltern:
You are impertinent. What has my husband to do with you? With a
woman like you?

Mrs Cheveley:
In this world like meets with like. It is because your husband is
himself fraudulent and dishonest that we pair so well together.
Between you and him there are chasms. He and I are closer than
friends. We are enemies linked together. The same sin binds us.

Lady Chiltern:
How dare you class my husband with yourself? How dare you
threaten him or me? Leave my house. You are unfit to enter it.

(Lord Chiltern enters)

Mrs Cheveley:
Your house! A house bought with the price of dishonour. A house,
everything in which has been paid for by fraud. Ask him what the
origin of his fortune is! Get him to tell you how he sold to a

stockbroker a Cabinet secret. Learn from him to what you owe your position.

<u>Lady Chiltern:</u>
(Sir Robert enters).
It is not true! Robert! It is not true!

<u>Mrs Cheveley:</u>
Look at him! Can he deny it? Does he dare to? I have not yet finished with you, with either of you. I give you both till tomorrow at noon. If by then you don't do what I bid you to do, the whole world shall know the origin of Robert Chiltern.

REALISM

Realism is a literary technique which describes locations, characters and themes in a realistic style without using elaborate imagery or rhetorical language. Literary realism emerged in the nineteenth century (circa 1870's) in France and was a popular modernist movement. The subjects and themes were of ordinary recognizable people, those characters readers could easily identify with. In drama, a set of theatrical conventions aim to create an illusion of reality on stage. Realism is still the dominant theatrical style today and is especially seen in film and TV.

Chekhov 1860-1904
Chekov is considered a master of realism.
His four major works are his plays: The Seagull, Uncle Vanya, The Three Sisters, and The Cherry Orchard. His play 'Ivanov' was based on an earlier play named 'The Wood Demon'. His three most popular plays, The Seagull, The Three Sisters and The Cherry Orchard were produced at Stanislavski's Moscow Arts Theatre.

Henrik Ibsen 1828-1906
Ibsen was Norwegian although he actually wrote his plays in Danish. He is a writer of realism and is often referred to as the 'father of realism'. Ibsen is known for his plays, 'Brand', 'Peer Gynt', 'An Enemy of the People', 'A Doll's House', 'Hedda Gabler,' 'Ghosts', 'The Wild Duck', 'The Master Builder'.

Ivan Turgenev 1818-1883
Russian novelist, poet and playwright. He was a contemporary of Dostoevsky and Tolstoy. Novels: Fathers & Sons, First love, Home of the Gentry. A Month in the Country was his only well-known theatre play and was originally known as The Student and later Two Women.

A MONTH IN THE COUNTRY
BY IVAN TURGENEV (1855)

(This 5 Act Russian play takes place on a country estate. 29 yr old, Natalia Petrovna is bored with her life as well as her husband. When a handsome 21 yr old suitor arrives to teach her young son, Kolia, Natalia falls in love with him. Unfortunately, so does the 17 yr old Vera).

Vera:
Did you want me, Natalia Petrovna?

Natalia:
Ah, Verochka!

Vera:
Do you feel quite well?

Natalia:
Perfectly, it's a little close that's all. Vera, I want to have a little talk with you ... A serious talk. Sit down my dear, will you? *(Vera sits)* Now... Vera, one thinks of you as still a child; but it is high time to give a thought to your future. You're an orphan and not a rich one at that: sooner or later you are bound to tire of living on somebody else's property. Now how would you like suddenly to have control of your very own house?

Vera:
I'm afraid I don't follow you, Natalia Petrovna ...

Natalia:
You are being sought in marriage. *(Vera stares at her - a pause)* You didn't expect this? I must confess I didn't either, you are still so young. I refuse to press you in the slightest - but I thought it my duty to let you know. *(As Vera suddenly covers her face with her hands)* Vera! My dear... what is it? But you're shaking like a leaf!

Vera:
Natalia Petrovna, I'm in your power…

Natalia:
In my power? Vera, what do you take me for? In my power indeed
- will you please take that back this minute? I command you! *(Vera
smiles).* That's better… Vera my child, I tell you what - you make
believe I'm your elder sister. Now one fine day your sister comes
to you and says, "What do you think little one? Somebody is
asking for your hand!" Well, what would be your first thought?

Vera:
I'd just say, "I'm too young".

Natalia:
Good; your sister would agree, the suitor would be given no for an
answer, fini … But suppose he was a very nice gentlemen with
means, prepared to bide his time … what then?

Vera:
Who is this suitor?

Natalia:
Ah, you're curious. Can't you guess?

Vera:
No.

Natalia:
Bolshinstov.

Vera:
Afanasy Ivanych?

Natalia:
Afanasy Ivanych. It's true he's not very young, and not wildly
prepossessing…

Vera:
You're joking…

Natalia:
No - but I see the matter is closed.

Vera:
I'm sorry but you took me completely by surprise… Do people still get married at his age?

Natalia:
But how old do you take him for? He's on the right side of fifty!

Vera:
I suppose he is, but he has such a peculiar face …

Natalia:
Bolshinstov, my dear, you are dead and buried, may you rest in peace … It was foolish of me to forget that little girl's dream of marrying for love.

Vera:
But, Natalia Petrovna … didn't you marry for love?

Natalia:
Yes, of course I did … eh bien fini! Bolshinstov, you are dismissed … There! And you're not frightened of me anymore?

Vera:
No, not any more …

Natalia:
Well then Verochka darling, just whisper quietly into my ear … you don't want to marry Bolshinstov because he's too old - but is that the only reason?

Vera:
Natalia Petrovna, isn't that reason enough?

Natalia:
Undoubtedly my dear… but you haven't answered my question.

Vera:
There is no other reason.

Natalia:
Oh… Of course, that puts the matter on rather a different footing.

Vera:
How do you mean, Natalia Petrovna?

Natalia:
I realize you can never fall in love with Bolshinstov; but he's an excellent man. And if there is nobody else … Isn't there anybody you're fond of?

Vera:
Well, there's you, and little Kolia …

Natalia:
Vera you must know what I mean … out of all the young men you've met … haven't you formed any attachment at all?

Vera:
I quite like one or two, but …

Natalia:
What about our philosopher, Rakitin?

Vera:
I'm very fond of him, of course, who wouldn't be …

Natalia:
An elder brother, I see… And the new tutor?

Vera:
Alexei Nikoliach?

Natalia:
Alexei Nikoliach.

Vera:
I like him very much.

Natalia:
He is nice, isn't he? Such a pity he's so bashful with everybody ...

Vera:
Oh, he isn't bashful with me!

Natalia:
Isn't he?

Vera:
I suppose it's because we're both orphans. I think he must appear shy to you because he's afraid of you. You see, he's had no chance to know you.

Natalia:
Afraid of me? How do you know?

Vera:
He told me so.

Natalia:
He told you ...

Vera:
Don't you like him, Natalia Petrovna?

Natalia:
He seems very kind-hearted.

Vera:
Oh he is! If only you knew ... The whole of this household loves him - he's so warm, once he's got over his shyness.

Natalia:
That doesn't sound a bit like him- when he's with me, he ...

Vera:
But that's what I mean, Natalia Petrovna, it's because he doesn't know you! I'll tell him how truly kind you are …

Natalia:
Thank you, my dear…

Vera:
You'll soon see the difference – because he listens to what I say, even though I am younger than he is …

Natalia:
I never knew you two were such good friends. You must be careful Vera.

Vera:
Careful?

Natalia:
I know he's a very pleasant young man, but at your age, it's not quite … people might think … but as you like him, and nothing more, then there is no real need for me to say another word, is there?

Vera:
He …

Natalia:
Vera is that the way you look at a sister? Those eyes are dying to tell me something … My poor Vera…

Vera:
Oh dear, I don't know what's the matter with me …

Natalia:
My poor sweet, and he… what of him?

Vera:
I don't know…

Natalia:
Vera, what of him?

Vera:
I don't know I tell you... sometimes I imagine ...

Natalia:
You imagine what?

Vera:
That I see a look in his eyes ... as if he thought of me as a special person, perhaps ... oh, I don't know ... What's the matter, Natalia Petrovna?

Natalia:
The matter... what did you say? Nothing ...

Vera:
But there is something the matter. I'll ring ...

Natalia:
No, no, don't ring ...

Vera:
You're not angry with me, Natalia Petrovna?

Natalia:
Not in the least, I just want to be by myself.

Vera:
Natalia Petrovna ...

Natalia:
Please ...

A DOLL'S HOUSE
BY HENRIK IBSEN (1879)

(Nora Helmer receives a visit from her old friend, Christine Linde, who has come to town looking for work. Nora confides in Christine that she has borrowed money in order to save her husband's poor health. Her husband is Helmer. She is very proud of the fact that she has been able to do this and means to repay the loan before anyone discovers it. However, later in the play, it is revealed that the signature on the loan has been forged and this results in Nora being blackmailed by the unscrupulous Krogstad).

Nora:
Oh, it's you, Christine. There's no one else outside, is there? Oh, I'm so glad you've come.

Mrs Linde:
I heard you were at my room asking for me.

Nora:
Yes. I want to ask you to help me with something. Let's sit down here on the sofa. Look at this. There is going to be a fancy-dress ball tomorrow night upstairs at Consul Stenborg's, and Torvald wants me to dance the tarantella.

Mrs Linde:
I say, are you going to give a performance?

Nora:
Yes, Torvald says I should.

Mrs Linde:
Is Dr Rank always in such low spirits as he was yesterday?

Nora:
No, last night it was very noticeable. But he's got a terrible disease – he's got spinal tuberculosis, poor man. His father was a frightful creature who kept mistresses and so on. As a result, Dr Rank has been sickly ever since he was a child.

Mrs Linde:
But, my dear Nora, how on earth did you get to know about such things?

Nora:
Oh, don't be silly, Christine – when one has three children, one comes into contact with women who know about medical matters - they tell one a thing or two.

Mrs Linde:
Does Dr Rank visit you every day?

Nora:
Yes, every day. He's Torvald's oldest friend, and a good friend to me too. Dr Rank's almost one of the family.

Mrs Linde:
But... is he perfectly sincere? Isn't he the kind of man that is very anxious to make himself agreeable?

Nora:
Yes, that's quite right, Christine. You see, Torvald's so hopelessly in love with me that he wants to have me all to himself. When we were first married, he got quite jealous if I as much as mentioned any of my old friends back home. So naturally, I stopped talking about them. But I often chat with Dr Rank about that kind of thing. He enjoys it, you see.

Mrs Linde:
Now listen, Nora. You ought to give up this business with Dr Rank.

Nora:
What business?

Mrs Linde:
Well, everything. Last night you were speaking about this rich admirer of yours who was going to give you money –

Nora:
Yes, who doesn't exist – unfortunately.

Mrs Linde:
Is Dr Rank rich?

Nora:
Yes.

Mrs Linde:
And he has no dependents?

Nora:
No, no one.

Mrs Linde:
And he comes here to see you every day? Tell me – is he quite sincere? I mean, doesn't he rather say the sort of thing he thinks people want to hear?

Nora:
No, quite the contrary. Whatever gave you that idea?

Mrs Linde:
But how dare a man of his education be so forward?

Nora:
What on earth are you talking about?

Mrs Linde:
Oh, stop pretending, Nora. Do you think I haven't guessed who it was who loaned you that two hundred pounds?

Nora:
Are you out of your mind? How could you imagine such a thing? A friend, someone who comes here every day!

Mrs Linde:
Then it really wasn't him?

Nora:
No, of course not. I've never for a moment dreamed of – anyway, he hadn't any money to lend then. I could never have dreamed of asking Dr Rank – though I'm sure, that if ever I did ask him –

Mrs Linde:
But of course, you won't.

Nora:
Of course not. I can't imagine that it should ever become necessary. But I'm perfectly sure that if I did speak to Dr Rank –

Mrs Linde:
Behind your husband's back?

Nora:
I've got to get out of this other business – and that's been going on behind his back. I've got to get out of it.

Mrs Linde:
Yes, that's what I told you yesterday.

——

Nora:
It's much easier for a man to arrange these things than a woman –

Mrs Linde:
One's own husband, yes.

Nora:
When you've completely repaid a debt, you get your I.O.U back, don't you?

Mrs Linde:
Yes, of course.

Nora:
And you can tear it into a thousand pieces and burn the filthy, beastly thing!

Mrs Linde:
Nora, you're hiding something from me.

Nora:
Can you see that?

Mrs Linde:
Something has happened since yesterday morning. What is it?

HEDDA GABLER ACT 1 (1890)
BY HENRIK IBSEN

(The scene takes place at the Tesman's new home. George Tesman and Hedda have recently returned from their six-month honeymoon. Mrs Elvsted is visiting Hedda. She has come to town to search of Eilert Loevborg. Mrs Elvsted knows Eilert as a tutor to her step-children whilst Hedda has had a previous romantic relationship with him. Hedda is very manipulative and is keen to 'quiz' the less than confident Thea Elvsted).

Mrs Elvsted:
I think I ought to be going now.

Hedda:
There's no hurry. *(Pause).* Well? How are things at home?

Mrs Elvsted:
I'd rather not speak about that.

Hedda:
But, my dear, you can tell me. Good heavens, we were at school together.

Mrs Elvsted:
Yes, but you were a year senior to me. I used to be terribly frightened of you in those days.

Hedda:
Frightened of me?

Mrs Elvsted:
Yes. Whenever you met me on the staircase you used to pull my hair. And once you said you'd burn it all off. And then afterwards – I mean, we've drifted so far apart. Our backgrounds were so different.

Hedda:
Well, now we must try to drift together again. Now listen. When we were at school, we used to call each other by our Christian names

Mrs Elvsted:
No, I'm sure you're mistaken.

Hedda:
I'm sure I'm not. I remember it quite clearly. Let's tell each other our secrets, as we used to in the old days. *(She moves closer to Mrs Elvsted).* There, now. You must call me Hedda.

Mrs Elvsted:
Oh, you're so kind. I'm not used to people being so nice to me.

Hedda:
Now, now. I shall call you Tora, the way I used to.

Mrs Elvsted:
My name is Thea.

Hedda:
Yes, of course. Of course, I meant Thea. So, you're not used to kindness, Thea? In your own home?

Mrs Elvsted:
Oh, if only I had a home! But I haven't. I've never had one.

Hedda:
I can't remember exactly, but didn't you first go to Mr Elvsted as a housekeeper?

Mrs Elvsted:
Governess, actually. But his wife – at the time, - she was an invalid, and had to spend most of her time in bed. So, I had to look after the house, too.

Hedda:
But in the end, you became mistress of the house.

Mrs Elvsted: *(sadly).*
Yes, I did.

Hedda:
Let me see. Roughly how long ago was that?

Mrs Elvsted:
When I got married, you mean?

Hedda:
Yes.

Mrs Elvsted:
About five years. Oh, those five years! Especially the last two or three. Oh, Mrs Tesman, if you only knew!

Hedda:
Mrs Tesman? Oh, Thea!

Mrs Elvsted:
I'm sorry. Yes – Hedda.

Hedda: *(casually)*.
Eilert Loevborg's been up there, too, for about three years, hasn't he?

Mrs Elvsted:
Eilert Loevborg? Yes, he has.

Hedda:
Did you know him before? When you were here?

Mrs Elvsted:
No, not really. I knew him by name, of course.

Hedda:
But up there, he used to visit you?

Mrs Elvsted:
Yes, he used to come and see us every day. To give the children lessons. I found I couldn't do that as well as manage the house.

Hedda:
I'm sure you couldn't. And your husband? I suppose being a magistrate he has to be away from home a good deal?

Mrs Elvsted:
Yes. You see, Mrs Tes – you see, Hedda, he has to cover the whole district.

Hedda:
Poor pretty little Thea! Now you must tell me the whole story. From beginning to end.

Mrs Elvsted:
Well, what do you want to know?

Hedda:
What kind of a man is your husband, Thea? I mean, as a person. Is he kind to you?

Mrs Elvsted:
I'm sure he does his best to be.

Hedda:
I only wonder if he isn't too old for you. There's more than twenty years between you, isn't there?

Mrs Elvsted:
Yes. Oh, there are so many things. We're different in every way. We've nothing in common. Nothing whatever.

Hedda:
But he loves you, surely? In his own way?

Mrs Elvsted:
Oh, I don't know. I think he finds me useful. And I don't cost much to keep.

Hedda:
Now you're being stupid.

Mrs Elvsted:
He doesn't love anyone except himself. And perhaps the children
– a little.

Hedda:
He must be fond of Eilert Loevborg, Thea.

Mrs Elvsted:
Eilert Loevborg? What makes you think that?

Hedda:
Well, if he sends you all the way down here to look for him –

Mrs Elvsted:
Well, I might as well tell you the whole story. It's bound to come
out sooner or later. My husband had no idea I was coming here.

Hedda:
What? Your husband didn't know?

Mrs Elvsted:
No, of course not. As a matter of fact, he wasn't even there. He
was away at the assizes. Oh, I couldn't stand it any longer,
Hedda! I'd be so dreadfully lonely up there now.

Hedda:
Go on.

Mrs Elvsted:
So, I packed a few things. Secretly. And went.

Hedda:
Without telling anyone?

Mrs Elvsted:
Yes. I caught the train and came straight here.

Hedda:
How brave of you!

Mrs Elvsted:
Well, what else could I do?

Hedda:
But what do you suppose your husband will say when you get back?

Mrs Elvsted:
Back there? To him? I shall never go back to him.

Hedda:
You mean you've left your home for good?

Mrs Elvsted:
Yes. I didn't see what else I could do.

Hedda:
But to do it so openly!

Mrs Elvsted:
Oh, it's no use trying to keep a thing like that secret.

Hedda:
But what do you suppose people will say?

Mrs Elvsted:
They can say what they like. I had to do it.

Hedda:
What do you intend to do now? How are you going to live?

Mrs Elvsted:
I don't know. I only know that I must live wherever Eilert Loevborg is. If I am to go on living.

Hedda:
Tell me, Thea, how did this – friendship between you and Eilert Loevborg begin?

Mrs Elvsted:
Oh, it came about gradually. I developed a kind of – power over him. He gave up his old habits. Not because I asked him to. I'd never have dared to do that. I suppose he just noticed I didn't like that kind of thing. So, he gave it up.

Hedda:
So, you've made a new man of him! Clever little Thea!

Mrs Elvsted:
Yes – anyway, he says I have. And he's made a – real person of me. Taught me to think – and to understand all kinds of things.

Hedda:
Did he give you lessons, too?

Mrs Elvsted:
Not exactly lessons. But he talked to me. About – oh, you've no idea – so many things! And then he let me work with him. Oh, it was wonderful. I was so happy to be allowed to help him.

Hedda:
Did he allow you to help him?

Mrs Elvsted:
Yes. Whenever he wrote anything we always – did it together.

Hedda:
Like good friends?

Mrs Elvsted:
Friends! Yes – why, Hedda, that's exactly the word he used! Oh, I ought to feel so happy. But I can't. I don't know if it will last.

Hedda:
You don't seem very sure of him.

Mrs Elvsted: (sadly).
Something stands between Eilert Loevborg and me. The shadow of another woman.

116

Hedda:
Who can that be?

Mrs Elvsted:
I don't know. Someone he used to be friendly with – someone he's never been able to forget.

Hedda:
What has he told you about her?

Mrs Elvsted:
He said when he left her, she tried to shoot him with a pistol.

Hedda: *(cold & controlled).*
What nonsense. People don't do such things.

Mrs Elvsted:
No. I think it must have been that red-haired singer he used to –

Hedda:
Ah yes, very probably.

Mrs Elvsted:
I remember they used to say she always carried a loaded pistol.

Hedda:
Well then, it must be her.

Mrs Elvsted:
But, Hedda, I hear she's come back and is living here. Oh, I'm so desperate !

Hedda:
Ssh! Tesman's coming. Thea, we mustn't breathe a word about this to anyone.

UNCLE VANYA ACT 2
BY ANTON CHEKHOV (1890)

(Sonya and Yeliena have a heart to heart and try to resolve their past differences).

Yeliena:
The storm's over. What wonderful air. (*Pause*) Where's the doctor?

Sonya:
Gone home.

Yeliena:
Sonya?

Sonya:
What?

Yeliena:
When are you going to stop sulking? We've done each other no harm, so why should we be enemies? Can't we call it off?

Sonya:
I've wanted to myself. (*She kisses her).* Let's not be angry anymore.

Yeliena:
That's splendid. (*They are both touched).*

Sonya:
Has father gone to bed?

Yeliena:
No, he's in the drawing-room. We don't speak to each other for weeks on end and heaven knows why. Let's drink to our friendship.

Sonya:
Yes, let's.

Yeliena:
From the same glass. (*She fills a glass*). That's better. So, we're friends now, Sonya?

Sonya:
Friends, Yeliena. (*They drink together and hug*). I've wanted to make it up for ages, but I felt too embarrassed somehow. (*She cries*).

Yeliena:
But why are you crying?

Sonya:
Never mind, it's nothing.

Yeliena:
There, there, that'll do. (*She cries*). You silly girl, now I'm crying too. (*Pause*) You're angry with me because you think I married your father for selfish reasons. I give you my word of honour, if that means anything to you, that I married him for love. He attracted me as a scholar and public figure. It wasn't real love, it was quite artificial, but it seemed real enough at the time. It wasn't my fault. But since the day we were married you've been tormenting me by looking as if you knew what I was up to and didn't much like it.

Sonya:
Please, please, remember we're friends now. Let's forget all that.

Yeliena:
You shouldn't look at people like that, it doesn't suit you. One must trust people or life becomes impossible. (*Pause*).

Sonya:
Tell me honestly, as a friend. Are you happy?

Yeliena:
No.

Sonya:
I knew it. Another question. Tell me frankly, do you wish you were married to somebody younger?

Yeliena:
What a child you are. Of course, I do. (*She laughs*) All right, ask me something else, go on.

Sonya:
Do you like the doctor?

Yeliena:
Yes, I do, very much.

Sonya:
I have a foolish expression on my face, haven't I? He's just left, but I can still hear his voice and footsteps. And if I look into a dark window I seem to see his face in it. Let me finish what I have to say. But I can't say it out loud like this, I feel too embarrassed. Let's go to my room and talk there. Do you think I'm silly? You do, don't you? Tell me something about him.

Yeliena:
Alright.

Sonya:
He's so intelligent. He can do anything, he's so clever. He practices medicine, plants trees –

Yeliena:
There's a bit more to it than medicine and trees. Don't you see, my dear? He's a brilliant man. And you know what that means? It means he has courage, flair, tremendous vision. When he plants a tree, he's already working out what the result will be in a thousand years' time, already glimpsing man's future happiness. People like that are rare and should be cherished. He drinks and is sometimes a bit rude, but never mind that. In Russia, a brilliant

man does his job and battles on, day in day out, in conditions like these, you can't expect that at the age of forty he'll still be a good little boy who doesn't drink. *(She kisses her).* I wish you happiness with all my heart. You deserve it. (*She stands up).* As for me, I'm just a tiresome character and not a very important one. In my music, in my husband's house, in all my romantic affairs – in everything – I've always played a minor role. Come to think of it, Sonya, I'm really very, very unhappy. (*She walks up and down in agitation).* There is no happiness for me in this world. None at all. What are you laughing at?

Sonya:
I'm so happy. So happy.

Yeliena:
I feel like playing the piano. I'd like to play something now.

Sonya:
Yes, do. I can't sleep. Do play something.

Yeliena:
Just a minute, your father is still awake. Music annoys him when he's unwell. Go and ask him and I'll play something if he doesn't mind. Go on.

Sonya:
Alright.

Yeliena:
It's ages since I played anything. I'll play and cry my eyes out like a silly girl.

THREE SISTERS ACT 1
BY ANTON CHEKHOV (1900)

(This is the opening scene of the play. Olga is reminiscing about the past and the fact that her father died exactly one year ago. Olga is dressed in her school teaching clothes. She is talking to her younger sister, Irina, who is dressed in white).

Olga:
It's been exactly one year since Father died – on your name day, Irina. It was bitter cold, snowing, remember? I didn't think I'd ever get through it. And you, you fainted dead away. But now a year has passed and it's easier to talk about. And you are wearing white again and you look radiant. (*She listens as the clock strikes*). The clock was striking then too. Remember, how the band was playing when they took father to the cemetery, how they fired a graveside salute? Hardly anyone came to the funeral and here he was a general, the commander of the brigade. Of course, it was raining and snowing heavily at the time._

Irina:
Why bring up old memories?

Olga:
It's so warm we can have the windows open and yet there is not a single bud on the birch trees. Eleven years ago, when father was given command of the brigade, we all came here from Moscow. I can remember perfectly the beginning of May in Moscow. By this time in Moscow everything's in full bloom, and it's warm – everything is bathed in sunlight. Eleven years have passed. But I remember everything as if we'd left yesterday. Oh, dear God! When I woke up this morning and saw the sunlight everywhere, I knew right away it was springtime, and I felt my heart would burst with joy! I wanted so much to go home again. (*She hears Masha whistling*). Don't whistle Masha. How can you? (*Pause*). After

teaching High School all day and then giving private lessons till dinner, I have a constant headache. And my thoughts – I've even started thinking like an old woman. In fact, for the past four years I've worked at the High School, every day I've felt my strength, my youth being drained off drop by drop. Only one thing, one dream keeps me strong, keeps me going … Moscow!

Irina:
To go to Moscow, to sell the house, have done with everything here and go to Moscow.

Olga:
Yes, to Moscow! As soon as we can.

Irina:
Andrei's probably going to be a professor and he won't live here anyway. There's nothing stopping us except poor Masha here.

Olga:
Masha can come and spend the whole summer in Moscow every year.

Irina:
I only pray it will work out all right. What a marvelous day! I'm in such a good mood, I don't know why. This morning I remembered it was my name-day and I suddenly felt happy, I remembered when we were children and Mother was still alive. And such wonderful thoughts passed through my head, I felt so excited.

Olga:
You're perfectly radiant today, I've never seen you look so beautiful. Masha's beautiful too. Andrei wouldn't be bad-looking either, only he's put on so much weight and it doesn't suit him. But I've aged and grown terribly thin – because I'm always losing my temper with the girls at school, I suppose. Now I have the day off,

I'm here at home, my headache's gone and I feel younger than I did yesterday. I'm twenty-eight, that's all. All's right with the world, but I think if I got married and stayed at home all day it might be even better. (*Pause*) I'd love my husband.

THREE SISTERS ACT 3
BY ANTON CHEKHOV (1900)

(Irina is feeling depressed and feels she will never get to Moscow or meet the man of her dreams).

Irina:
It's true, how small minded our Andrei has become. How he's wasted himself and grown old, living with that woman! There was a time when he was aiming to be a professor, but now, only yesterday he was boasting that he's at last managed to be elected as a member of the local district council. He's a member of the council, and Protopopov is Chairman … the whole town is talking about it and laughing at him, but he is the only one who knows nothing and sees nothing … Just now everyone ran to help to fight the fire, but *he* sat alone in his study and did not give it a thought. He just plays on the violin. It's terrible, terrible, terrible! (*She cries*) It's too much for me, I can't bear it any longer! … I can't, I can't …. (*She sobs bitterly*).

Olga:
But what's the matter, darling?

Irina:
Don't have anything more to do with me, don't, don't, I can't bear it any longer! (*Sobbing*). Where? Where has it all gone? Where is it? Oh my God, my God! I have forgotten everything, forgotten everything … Everything is confused in my head … I can't remember what is the word for window in Italian, for ceiling … I am forgetting everything. I forget more every day, and life flies past and never returns, never, and we will never go to Moscow … I see now that we will never go …. (*gaining some control*).

Olga:
Don't, dear, don't.

Irina:
Oh, I'm so unhappy … I can't work, I won't work. That's enough! I used to work in the Telegraph Office, now I am employed by the Town Council, and I hate and despise everything that they give me to do … I'm already twenty-four, I have been working already for ages, my brain is drying up, I'm growing ugly and old, and nothing I do, nothing at all gives me any joy, and time flies by and all the time it seems as if you are abandoning real life, life that is beautiful, you are going farther and farther away from it, over some sort of precipice. I am in total despair, and how I am alive, why I have not killed myself before now I don't understand… I won't cry, I won't cry… That's enough! …Look, I've already stopped crying. That's enough… enough! I kept on waiting, thinking we would settle in Moscow, and there my ideal man would meet me. I dreamed about him, I loved him …But it turns out it was all nonsense, all nonsense ….

Olga:
Don't cry, child, please, it upsets me so.

Irina:
I'm not crying. I'm not. I won't. Look, I've stopped now. I must stop, I really must.

Olga:
My dear, let me tell you something as your sister and your friend. If you want my advice, marry the baron. *(Irina continues crying).* After all you do respect him, you think so much of him. He may not be all that good-looking, but he's a fine, decent man. One doesn't marry for love, you know, it's only a matter of doing one's duty. That's what I think anyway, and I'd marry without love. I'd marry the first man who came along provided it was someone honest and decent. I'd even marry an old man.

Irina:

I've been waiting for us to move to Moscow all this time, thinking I'd meet my true love there. I've dreamed about him, loved him, but that was sheer foolishness as it's turned out.

Olga:

I understand, Irina darling, I do understand. When the baron resigned his commission and came to see us in his civilian suit, he looked so ugly - it actually brought tears to my eyes. He asked me why I was crying. How could I tell him? But if he did marry you, if such was God's will, I'd be happy. That's an altogether different thing, you see.

THE CHERRY ORCHARD ACT 1
BY ANTON CHEKHOV (1903)

(Anya has recently arrived home from Paris with her mother, Madame Ranevsky. She catches up with her adopted sister, Varya).

Varya:
Well, thank heavens you're back. You're home again. My lovely darling, Anya's home again.

Anya:
I've had a terrible time.

Varya:
I can imagine.

Anya:
I left just before Easter and it was cold then. On the way there, Charlotte kept talking and doing those awful tricks of hers. Why you ever landed me with Charlotte …

Varya:
But you couldn't have gone on your own, darling. A girl of seventeen.

Anya:
It was cold and snowing when we got to Paris. My French is atrocious. I find Mother living on the fourth floor somewhere and when I get there, she has visitors, French people – some ladies and an old priest with a little book. The place is full of smoke and awfully uncomfortable. Suddenly I felt sorry for Mother, so sorry, I took her head in my arms and held her and just couldn't let go. Afterwards, Mother was terribly sweet to me and kept crying.

Varya:
Don't, Anya. I can't bear it.

Anya:
She'd already sold her villa near Menton and had nothing left, nothing at all. I hadn't any money either, there was hardly enough for the journey. And Mother simply won't understand. If we have a meal in a station restaurant, she asks for all the most expensive things and tips the waiters a rouble each. And Charlotte's no better. Then Yasha has to have his share as well, it was simply awful. Mother has this servant, Yasha, you know, we've brought him with us …

Varya:
Yes, I've seen him. Isn't he foul?

Anya:
Yes. Well, how is everything? Have you paid the interest?

Varya:
What a hope!

Anya:
My God, how dreadful.

Varya:
The estate is up for sale in August.

Anya:
Oh my God! *(Pause).* Has Lopakhin proposed, Varya? But he does love you. Why can't you get it all settled? What are you both waiting for?

Varya:
I don't think anything will come of it. He's so busy he can't be

bothered with me. He doesn't even notice me. Wretched man, I'm fed up with the sight of him. Everyone's talking about our wedding and congratulating us, when there's nothing in it at all actually and the whole thing's so vague. *(Changing the subject).* You've got a brooch that looks like a bee or something.

Anya:
Yes, Mother bought it. Do you know, in Paris, I went up in a balloon.

Varya:
My lovely, darling Anya's home again. You know, darling, while I'm doing my jobs around the house, I spend the whole day dreaming. I imagine marrying you off to a rich man. That would set my mind at rest and I'd go off to a convent, then on to Kiev and Moscow, wandering from one holy place to another. I'd just wander on and on. What bliss!

Anya:
The bird's are singing in the orchard. What time is it?

Varya:
It must be nearly three. Time you were asleep, dear. What bliss!

GEORGE BERNARD SHAW
IRISH DRAMATIST
1856-1950

G B Shaw was an Irish playwright born in Dublin. He criticized mainstream education and had an aversion to schools and teachers. He moved to England is 1876. He was also a music and literary critic, journalist and polemicist. He was the winner of an Academy Award and a Nobel Prize for Literature (1925). He wrote essays, short stories and novels as well as a prolific number of plays.

Shaw wrote over 60 plays. They covered social themes such the class system, marriage and religion. He was a comedic writer as well as a socialist and addressed issues such as poverty, capitalism and women's rights. He wished to transform society through education.

His most well-known plays are: Pygmalion, Arms & The Man, Mrs Warren's Profession, Candida, Major Barbara, Heartbreak House, Saint Joan, Androcles & the Lion, Arms and the Man, You Never Can Tell & Back to Methuselah. His play 'Pygmalion' was adapted into the popular musical 'My Fair Lady'.

MRS WARREN'S PROFESSION ACT 2
BY G B SHAW (1902)

*(Mrs Warren is a former prostitute who has accumulated a lot of
wealth which has enabled her to educate her daughter, Vivie. Now
that Vivie has found out about her mother's past, she is very
disapproving and finds it difficult to forgive her. Her mother
explains her motives and Vivie is eventually able to comprehend
her mother's actions).*

Mrs Warren:
What do you know of men, child, to talk that way about them?
You'll have to make up your mind to see a good deal of Sir
George Crofts, as he's a friend of mine.

Vivie:
Why? Do you expect that we shall be much together? You and I, I
mean?

Mrs Warren:
Of course, until you're married.

Vivie:
Do you think my way of life would suit you?

Mrs Warren:
You and your way of life, indeed! I've been noticing these airs in
you and if you think I'm going to put up with them you're mistaken.

Vivie:
Everybody knows my reputations, my social standing, and the
profession I intend to pursue. I know nothing about you. What is
that way of life which you invite me to share with you and Sir
George Crofts?

Mrs Warren:
How can you be so hard on me? Have I no rights over you as your mother?

Vivie:
Are you my mother?

Mrs Warren:
I am your mother!

Vivie:
Then where are our relatives? My father? Our family friends? Who was my father?

Mrs Warren:
You don't know what you're asking. I can't tell you.

Vivie:
I have a right to know. You can refuse to tell me, if you please, but if you do, you will see the last of me tomorrow morning.

Mrs Warren:
My God, what sort of woman are you? What right have you to set yourself up above me like this? You boast of what you are to me – I, who gave you the chance of being what you are.

Vivie:
I shall always respect your right to your own opinions and your own way of life.

Mrs Warren:
Do you think I was brought up like you? Able to pick and choose my own way of life? Do you think I did what I did because I like it, or thought it right, or wouldn't rather have gone to college and been a lady if I'd had the chance?

Vivie:
Everybody has some choice, mother. The poorest girl alive can choose between rag-picking and flower-selling, according to her taste. People are always blaming their circumstances for what they are. I don't believe in circumstances. The people who get on in this world are the people who get up and look for the circumstances they want, and, if they can't find them, make them.

Mrs Warren:
Oh, it's easy to talk, very easy, isn't it? Would you like to know what my circumstances were? D'you know what your grandmother was?

Vivie:
No.

Mrs Warren:
She called herself a widow and had a fried-fish shop and kept herself and four daughters out of it. Two of us were sisters; that was me and Liz; and we were both good-looking and well made. The other two were only half sisters; undersized, starved looking, hard-working, honest poor creatures; they were the respectable ones. Liz and I went to a church school – that was part of the ladylike airs we gave ourselves to be superior to the children that knew nothing and went nowhere – and we stayed there until Liz went out one night and never came back. I became a waitress; then I went to a bar at Waterloo station; One cold, wretched night, when I was so tired, I could hardly keep myself awake, who should come up for half of Scotch but Lizzie, in a long fur cloak, elegant and comfortable, with a lot of sovereigns in her purse. When she saw that I'd grown up good-looking she said to me across the bar, 'What are you doing there, you little fool? Wearing out your health and your appearance for other people's profit!' And then I went into business with her as her partner. The house in Brussels was real high class; a much better place for a woman

134

to be in than the factory where Anne Jane got poisoned. Would you have had me become a worn-out old drudge before I was forty?

Vivie:
No; but why did you choose that business? Saving money and good management will succeed in any business.

Mrs Warren:
All we had was our appearance and our turn for pleasing men. What is any respectable girl brought up to do but to catch some rich man's fancy and get the benefit of his money by marrying him? As if a marriage ceremony could make any difference in the right or wrong of the thing! Oh, the hypocrisy of the world makes me sick!

Vivie:
You are stronger than all England. And are you really and truly not one wee bit doubtful – or – ashamed?

Mrs Warren:
It's only good manners to be ashamed of it; Women have to pretend to feel a great deal that they don't feel.

Vivie:
You have got completely the better of me tonight, though I intended it to be the other way. Let us be good friends now. Goodnight, dear old mother.

PYGMALION
BY GEORGE BERNARD SHAW (1914)

(In Act 2, Eliza Doolittle is taken to the third floor of Professor Higgins house in London by Mrs Pearce, the housekeeper. Mrs Pearce shows Eliza her new room where she is to stay whilst she is under Professor Higgins tuition. Higgins experiment is to turn the Cockney flower-seller, Eliza, into a 'lady').

<u>Mrs Pearce:</u>
I will have to put you here. This will be your bedroom.

<u>Liza:</u>
Oh, I couldn't sleep here, missus. It's too good for the likes of me. I should be afraid to touch anything. I aint a duchess yet, you know.

<u>Mrs Pearce:</u>
You have got to make yourself as clean as the room: then you won't be afraid of it. And you must call me Mrs Pearce, not missus. *(She shows Eliza the bathroom).*

<u>Liza:</u>
Gawd! What's this? Is this where you wash clothes? Funny sort of copper, I call it.

<u>Mrs Pearce:</u>
It is not a copper. This is where we wash ourselves, Eliza, and where I am going to wash you.

<u>Liza:</u>
You expect me to get into that and wet myself all over! Not me. I should catch my death. I knew a woman did it every Saturday night; and she died of it.

<u>Mrs Pearce:</u>
Mr Higgins has the gentlemen's bathroom downstairs; and he has a bath every morning, in cold water.

Liza:
Ugh! He's made of iron, that man.

Mrs Pearce:
If you are to sit with him and the Colonel and be taught you will have to do the same. They won't like the smell of you if you don't. But you can have the water as hot as you like. There are two taps: hot and cold.

Liza: *(weeping).*
I couldn't. It's not natural: it would kill me. I've never had a bath in my life: not what you'd call a proper one.

Mrs Pearce:
Well, don't you want to be clean and sweet and decent, like a lady? You know you can't be a nice girl inside if you're a dirty slut outside. *(Liza continues wailing).* Now stop crying and go back into your room and take off all your clothes. Then wrap yourself in this *(she gives her a dressing gown).* and come back to me. I will get the bath ready.

Liza:
I can't. I won't. I'm not used to it. I've never took off all my clothes before. It's not right: it's not decent.

Mrs Pearce:
Nonsense, child. Don't you take off all your clothes every night when you go to bed?

Liza:
No. Why should I? I should catch my death. Of course, I take off my skirt.

Mrs Pearce:
Do you mean that you sleep in the underclothes you wear in the daytime?

Liza:
What else have I to sleep in?

Mrs Pearce:
You will never do that again as long as you live here. I will get you a proper nightdress.

Liza:
Do you mean change into cold things and lie awake shivering half the night? You want to kill me, you do.

Mrs Pearce:
I want to change you from a frowzy slut to a clean respectable girl fit to sit with the gentlemen in the study. Are you going to trust me and do what I tell you or be thrown out and sent back to your flower basket?

Liza:
But you don't know what the cold is to me. You don't know how I dread it.

Mrs Pearce:
Your bed won't be cold here. I will put a hot water bottle in it. *(She pushes Eliza into the bedroom).* Off with you and undress.

Liza:
Oh, if only I'd a known what a dreadful thing it is to be clean, I'd never had come. I didn't know when I was well-off. I –

(Mrs Pearce fills the bath, testing it with a bath thermometer. She adds perfumed bath salts. Eliza returns dressed in a bath robe).

Mrs Pearce:
Now come along. Take that thing off.

Liza:
Oh, I couldn't, Mrs Pearce: I really couldn't. I never done such a thing.

Mrs Pearce:
Nonsense. Here: step in and tell me whether it's hot enough for you.

Liza:
Ah! Oh! It's too hot.

Mrs Pearce:
It won't hurt you. *(Mrs Pearce pushes Eliza down into the bath and starts to work with the scrubbing brush whilst Eliza's screams are heartrending).*

JEAN ANOUILH 1910-1987

Jean Anouilh was a French dramatic who best known play is
Antigone. It is an adaption of Sophocles Greek tragedy and
Anouilh adapted it as a political attack on the government of the
time. His themes are often of integrity and morality although he
also wrote some farces. His father was a tailor and his mother was
a violinist who played in an orchestra to supplement the family
income. Anouilh later wrote a short play called 'The Orchestra'.
Anouilh often attended rehearsals with his mother and this is most
likely where he discovered his inspiration for playwrighting.
Anouilh studied at the Sorbonne but due to financial troubles cut
short his education and went to work at an advertising agency.
After being called for military service he married an actress who
performed in many of his plays. His play 'Antigone' is considered a
political parable and brought Anouilh much recognition. Other
well-known plays are: Romeo and Juliette, Medea and Joan of Arc
and Thomas Becket.

ANTIGONE BY JEAN ANOUILH (1942)

(Antigone's parents are dead and now King Creon is on the throne after Antigone's two brothers have killed each other in a civil battle. Creon has given one brother a decent burial whilst leaving the other to rot in the street for all to see. In this scene, Antigone is being questioned by her nurse. Her nurse has noticed that Antigone has been going out in the middle of the night. The nurse thinks she is meeting a boyfriend. The reason for her secret rendezvous is that Antigone is intent on giving her brother a decent burial so that he may find peace in the afterlife).

Nurse:
Where have you been?

Antigone:
Just out for a walk. It was all grey. Beautiful. But now, everything's turned pink and yellow and green. Like a postcard. You'll have to get up earlier, Nan, if you want to see a world without colours.

Nurse:
Not so fast! I went to your room to make sure you hadn't thrown the blankets off in your sleep … and the bed was empty!

Antigone:
The garden was still asleep. I caught it unawares. A garden that hasn't yet begun to think about people. Beautiful.

Nurse:
I soon saw you'd gone out – you'd left the back door open.

Antigone:
The fields were all wet. Waiting. Everything was waiting. I made a terrific noise all by myself on the road, and I felt awkward because I knew the waiting wasn't for me. So, I took my sandals off and melted into the landscape …

Nurse:
You're going to have to wash those feet before you get back into bed.

Antigone:
I'm not going back to bed.

Nurse:
Four o'clock. It wasn't even four o'clock yet! I get up to make sure she's still properly covered up, and there's her bed cold and nobody in it!

Antigone:
Do you think it would be like that every morning, being the first girl out?

Nurse:
Morning! Middle of the night you mean! And are you trying to tell me you were only out for a walk? Storyteller! Where've you been?

Antigone:
You're right. It was still night. I was the only one out there who thought it was morning. The first person today to believe in the light.

Nurse:
Go on then, play the fool. I'm up to all your tricks – I was young once myself and I was a handful too. Now tell me where you've been, you naughty girl!

Antigone:
I wasn't doing anything wrong.

Nurse:
You had a rendez-vous, I suppose, don't tell me you hadn't!

Antigone:
Yes, I had a rendezvous.

Nurse:
You mean, you've got a sweetheart?

Antigone:
Yes ... poor thing.

Nurse:
A nice thing for a king's daughter, I must say! You half kill yourself to bring them up, but they're all the same. Who is it? Some young layabout, I suppose? A boy you can't even introduce to your family as the one you love and want to marry? That's it, isn't it … isn't it? Answer me, you brazen hussy!

Antigone:
(Lying). Yes. Nurse. That's it.

Nurse:
And do you know what he's going to say when he hears about you getting up in the middle of the night? And what about Haemon, your fiancé? She's engaged, and she gets up at four in the morning to gad about with someone else! And then she wants to be left alone – her highness doesn't want anyone to say anything about it!

Antigone:
Don't make a fuss, Nan. You oughtn't to be too cross this morning.

Nurse:
Not make a fuss! When I think how I promised her mother … ! What would she say if she was here? "You silly old fool", she'd say "so you couldn't keep my little girl virtuous for me!" That's what your mother will say to me up there, when I go. And I'll be so ashamed I could die, if I wasn't dead already, and all I'll be able to do is to hang my head in shame and say, "Yes, Lady Jocasta – you're absolutely right".

Antigone:
Stop crying, Nan. You'll be able to look her straight in the eye, and she'll thank you for taking such good care of me. She knows why I went out this morning.

Nurse:
You haven't got a sweetheart?

Antigone:
No.

Nurse:
So, you've been making fun of me? I suppose it's because I'm old. You were always my favourite. And though your sister was easier to manage, I thought it was you who loved me best too. But if you did love me, you would have told me the truth. Why was your bed empty? When I came to tuck you in?

Antigone:
Please don't cry. Come along my little red apple. Do you remember when I used to rub your cheeks 'till they shone? Don't fill all these little furrows with tears for nothing. I am virtuous; I swear I have no other sweetheart than Haemon. If you like, I'll swear I never shall. Save your tears – you may have need of them. When you cry I feel like a little girl again. And I mustn't be little today.

ANTIGONE BY JEAN ANOUILH (1942)

(This scene is from Jean Anouilh's version of Sophocles Greek tragedy Antigone. Antigone is informing her younger sister, Ismene, that she intendeds to defy their uncle King Creon and bury her brother, Polynices. Polynices has been left to rot whilst their elder brother has been dignified with a decent burial. Ismene, Antigone's older sister, speaks with reason and tries to persuade her headstrong sister not to do it. She knows the penalty is death).

<u>Ismene:</u>
Aren't you well?

<u>Antigone:</u>
Of course, I am. Just a little tired. I got up too early.

<u>Ismene:</u>
I couldn't sleep either.

<u>Antigone:</u>
Ismene, you ought not to go without your beauty sleep.

<u>Ismene:</u>
Don't make fun of me.

<u>Antigone:</u>
I'm not Ismene truly.

<u>Ismene:</u>
Why do you insist upon talking about other things?

<u>Antigone:</u>
I'm not talking about other things.

<u>Ismene:</u>
Antigone, I've thought about it a lot.

<u>Antigone:</u>
Have you?

Ismene:
I thought about it all night long. Antigone, you're mad.

Antigone:
Am I?

Ismene:
We cannot do it.

Antigone:
Why not?

Ismene:
Creon will have us put to death.

Antigone:
Of course, he will. That's what he's here for. He will do what he has to do, and we will do what we have to do. He is bound to put us to death. We are bound to go out and bury our brother. That's the way it is. What do you think we can do to change it?

Ismene:
I don't want to die.

Antigone:
I'd prefer not to die, myself.

Ismene:
Listen to me, Antigone. I thought about it all night. I'm older than you are. I always think things over and you don't. You are impulsive. You get a notion in your head and you jump up and do the thing straight off. And if it's silly, well so much the worst for you. Where, I think things out.

Antigone:
Sometimes it is better not to think too much.

Ismene:
I don't agree with you! Oh, I know it's horrible. And I pity Polynices just as much as you do. But all the same, I sort of see what Uncle

Creon means.

Antigone:
I don't want to 'sort of see' anything.

Ismene:
Uncle Creon is the King. He has to set an example!

Antigone:
But I am not the King: and I don't have to set people examples.

Ismene:
Listen to me. I'm right oftener than you are.

Antigone:
I don't want to be right!

Ismene:
At least you can try to understand.

Antigone:
Understand! The first word I ever heard out of any of you was the word 'understand'. Understand! I don't want to understand. There'll be time enough when I'm old to understand … If I ever am old. But not now.

Ismene:
He is stronger than we are, Antigone. He is the King. And the whole city is with him. Thousands and thousands of them, swarming through all the streets of Thebes.

Antigone:
I am not listening to you.

Ismene:
His mob will come running, howling as it runs. A thousand arms will seize our arms. A thousand breaths will breathe into our faces. And we shall suffer, we shall feel pain rising in us until it becomes so unbearable that we know it must stop. But it won't stop: it will go on rising and rising, like a screaming voice. Oh, I can't, I can't,

Antigone.

Antigone:
How well you have thought it all out.

Ismene:
I thought of it all night long. Didn't you?

Antigone:
Oh, yes.

Ismene:
I'm an awful coward, Antigone.

Antigone:
So am I. But what has that got to do with it?

Ismene:
Don't you want to go on living?

Antigone:
Go on living? Who was it that was always the first out of bed because she loved the touch of the cold morning air on her bare skin? Who was always the last to bed because nothing less than infinite weariness could wean her from the lingering night?

Ismene:
Darling little sister!

Antigone:
No! For heaven's sake! Don't paw me! And don't let us start snivelling! You say you've thought it all out. The howling mob, the torture, the fear of death … They've made up your mind for you. Is that it?

Ismene:
Yes.

Antigone:
All right. They're as good excuses as any.

Ismene:
Antigone, be sensible. It's all very well for men to believe in ideas and die for them. But you're a girl!

Antigone:
Don't I know I am a girl? Haven't I spent the whole of my life cursing the fact that I was a girl?

Ismene:
Antigone! You have everything in the world to make you happy. You are going to be married; you are young; you are beautiful …

Antigone:
I am not beautiful.

Ismene:
Yes, you are! And what about Haemon?

Antigone:
I shall see Haemon this morning. I'll take care of Haemon. Go back to bed now Ismene. The sun is coming up, and, as you can see there is nothing I can do today. Our brother Polynices is as well guarded as if he had won the war and were sitting on his throne.

Ismene:
What are you going to do?

Antigone:
I don't feel like going to bed. However, if you like, I'll promise not to leave the house till you wake up. Go and get some sleep. Look at you: you can hardly keep your eyes open. Go!

Ismene:
And you will listen to reason, won't you? Let me talk to you about this again? Promise?

Antigone:
I promise. I'll let you talk. I'll let all of you talk. Go to bed now.

TENNESSEE WILLIAMS
1911-1983

American Pulitzer winning playwright. His works include 'A
Streetcar named Desire', The Glass Menagerie', 'Cat on a Hot Tin
Roof' and 'Camino Real'. They have all been adapted into films of
note. His family background providing themes for his plays. He
was brought up by his mother and an absent father who preferred
work to family life. He studied journalism at Missouri University but
was pulled out when his father discovered that his girlfriend was
studying there too. Tennessee (not his real name but the town
from where his father originated) returned home and went to work,
writing in his spare time, but soon suffered a nervous breakdown.
He later made friends with a group of poets and returned to Iowa
university from where he eventually graduated. At the age of 28,
he moved to New Orleans and wrote A Streetcar Named Desire.
His reputation grew and he started writing scripts for MGM. He
preferred writing for the theatre however, and later his plays were
staged on Broadway. During the 60's, Williams work was less
prolific and he turned to drugs and alcohol and eventually died of
a stroke in New York City.

A STREETCAR NAMED DESIRE (1947)
BY TENNESSEE WILLIAMS

(30 yr old Blanche Dubois is visiting her sister, 25yr old Stella Kowalski, in the slums of New Orleans. Blanche is a former school teacher with a hidden secret. Blanche has outstayed her welcome and Stella's husband, Stanley, is losing his patience. In this scene, Blanche is questioning Stella over what people around her are saying).

Blanche:
Stella! What have you heard about me? What have people been telling you about me?

Stella:
Telling?

Blanche:
You haven't heard any – unkind – gossip about me?

Stella:
Why, no, Blanche, of course not!

Blanche:
Honey, there was – a good deal of talk in Laurel.

Stella:
About you, Blanche?

Blanche:
I wasn't so good the last two years or so, after Belle Reve had started to slip through my fingers.

Stella:
All of us do things we –

Blanche:
I never was hard or self-sufficient enough. When people are soft – soft people have got to court the favour of hard ones, Stella. Have got to be seductive – put on soft colours, the colours of butterfly

wings, - make a little – temporary magic just in order to pay for – one night's shelter. That's why I've been – not so awf'ly good lately. I've run for protection, Stella, from under one leaky roof to another leaky roof. People don't see you – men don't – don't even admit your existence unless they are making love to you. And you've got to have your existence admitted by someone, if you're going to have someone's protection. I don't know how much longer I can turn the trick. I'm fading now! *(Pause).* Have you been listening to me?

Stella:
I don't listen to you when you are being morbid! *(Stella offers Blanche a coke).*

Blanche:
Is that coke for me?

Stella:
Not for anyone else!

Blanche:
Why you precious thing. Is it just coke?

Stella:
You mean you want a shot in it?

Blanche:
Well, honey, a shot never does a coke any harm! Let me? You mustn't wait on me!

Stella:
I like to wait on you, Blanche. It makes it seem more like home.

Blanche:
I have to admit I love to be waited on … You're so good to me! And I – I know. You hate me to talk sentimental. But honey, believe I feel things more than I tell you. I won't stay long! I promise …

Stella:
Blanche.

Blanche:
I won't, I promise, I'll go. Go soon! I will really! I won't hang around
until he – throws me out …

Stella:
Now will you stop talking foolish?

Blanche:
Yes, honey. Watch how you pour – right on my pretty white skirt!
(*Blanche screams*).

Stella:
Oh … Use my hanky. Blot gently. Did it stain?

Blanche:
Not a bit. Isn't that lucky?

Stella:
Why did you scream like that?

Blanche:
I don't know why I screamed! Mitch – Mitch is coming at seven. I
guess I'm just feeing nervous about our relations. He hasn't gotten
a thing but a good-night kiss, that's all I have given him, Stella. I
want his respect. And men don't want anything they get too easy.
But on the other hand, men lose interest quickly. Especially when
the girl is over – thirty. They think a girl over thirty ought to – the
vulgar term is – 'put out' … And I – I'm not 'putting out'. Of course,
he – he doesn't know – I mean I haven't informed him – of my real
age!

Stella:
Why are you so sensitive about your age?

Blanche:
Because of hard knocks my vanity's been given. What I mean is –
he thinks I'm sort of – prim and proper, you know! (*she laughs*

sharply). I want to deceive him enough to make him want me …

Stella:
Blanche, do you want him?

Blanche:
I want to rest! I want to breathe quietly again! Yes – I want Mitch … very badly! Just think! If it happens! I can leave here and not be anyone's problem …

Stella:
(She kisses her sister impulsively). It will happen!

Blanche:
(Doubtfully). It will?

Stella:
It will! It will, honey … but don't take another drink!

(She goes out of the door to meet her husband, Stanley).

THE GLASS MENGAGERIE BY TENNESSEE WILLIAMS (1944)

(Amanda has brought up her two children alone after her husband left her. Laura wears her leg in a brace and is painfully shy. In Scene 2, Amanda, Laura's mother, appears on the fire escape steps. On hearing her mother returning, Laura, thrusts the bowl of glass ornaments away and sits before the typewriter keyboard. She has a confession to make after her dropping out of business college is discovered).

Laura:
Hello, Mother, I was –

Amanda:
Deception? Deception? (*She slowly removes her hat and gloves*).

Laura:
How was the D.A.R. meeting? Didn't you go to the D.A.R. meeting, Mother?

Amanda:
No – I did not have the strength – to go to the D.A.R. In fact, I did not have the courage! I wanted to find a hole in the ground and hide myself in it forever! How old are you, Laura?

Laura:
Mother, you know my age.

Amanda:
I thought you were an adult; it seems that I was mistaken.

Laura:
Please don't stare at me, Mother.

Amanda:
What are we going to do, what is going to become of us, what is the future?

Laura:
Has something happened Mother?

Amanda:
I'll be all right in a minute, I'm just bewildered – by life ...

Laura:
Mother, I wish that you would tell me what's happened!

Amanda:
As you know, I was supposed to be inducted into my office at the D.A.R. this afternoon. But I stopped off at Rubicam's business college to speak to your teachers about your having a cold and ask them what progress they thought you were making down there.

Laura:
Oh ...

Amanda:
I went to the typing instructor and introduced myself as your mother. She didn't know who you were. Wingfield, she said. We don't have any such student enrolled at the school! I assured her she did, that you had been going to classes since early in January. "I wonder", she said, "if you could be talking about that terribly shy little girl who dropped out of school after only a few days attendance?" "No," I said, 'Laura, my daughter, has been going to school every day for the past six weeks!" "Excuse me," she said. She took the attendance book out and there was your name, unmistakably printed, and all the dates you were absent until they decided that you had dropped out of school. I still said, "No, there must have been some mistake. There must have been some mix-up in the records!" And she said, "No – I remember her perfectly now. Her hands shook so that she couldn't hit the right keys! The first time we gave a speed-test, she broke down completely – was sick at the stomach and almost had to be carried into the washroom! After that morning she never showed up anymore. We phoned the house but never got any answer". I felt so weak I could barely keep on my feet! I had to sit down while they got me a glass of water! Fifty dollars' tuition, all of our plans –

my hopes and ambition for you. What are you doing? Where have you been going when you've gone on pretending that you were going to business college?

Laura:
I've just been going out walking.

Amanda:
Walking? In winter? Deliberately courting pneumonia in that light coat? Where did you walk to, Laura?

Laura:
All sorts of places – mostly in the park. I couldn't go back. I – threw up – on the floor!

Amanda:
From half past seven 'till after five every day you mean to tell me you walked around in the park, because you wanted to make me think that you were still going to Rubicam's Business College?

Laura:
It wasn't as bad as it sounds. I went inside places to get warmed up. I went in the art museum and the birdhouses at the Zoo. I visited the penguins every day! Sometimes I did without lunch and went to the movies. Lately, I've been spending most of my afternoons in the Jewel-box, the big glasshouse where they raise the tropical flowers.

Amanda:
You did all this to deceive me, just for deception? Why?

Laura:
Mother, when you're disappointed, you get that awful suffering look on your face, like the picture of Jesus' mother in the museum! I couldn't face it.

Amanda:
So. what are we going to do the rest of our lives? Stay home and watch the parades go by? Amuse ourselves with the glass menagerie, darling? Eternally play those worn-out phonograph

records your father left as a painful reminder of him? What is there left but dependency all our lives? I know so well what becomes of unmarried women who aren't prepared to occupy a position. Is that the future that we've mapped out for ourselves? Of course – some girls do marry. Haven't you ever liked some boy?

Laura:
Yes. I liked one once. I came across his picture a while ago.

Amanda:
He gave you his picture?

Laura:
No, it's in the year-book.

Amanda:
Oh – a high-school boy.

Laura:
His name was Jim. Here he is in the Pirates of Penzance. The operetta the senior class put on. He had a wonderful voice and we sat across the aisle from each other Mondays, Wednesdays, and Fridays in the Auditorium. Here he is with the silver cup for debating! See his grin?

Amanda:
He must have had a jolly disposition.

Laura:
He used to call me – Blue Roses.

Amanda:
Why did he call you such a name as that?

Laura:
When I had that attack of pleurosis – he asked me what was the matter. When I came back, I said pleurosis – he thought that I said Blue Roses! So that's what he always called me after that. Whenever he saw me, he'd holler 'Hello, Blue Roses!' I didn't care for the girls he went out with. Emily Meisenback. Emily was the

best-dressed girl at Soldan. She never struck me, though, as being sincere … It says in the Personal Section – they're engaged. That's six years ago! They must be married by now.

Amanda:
Girls that aren't cut out for business careers usually wind up married to some nice man. Sister, that's what you'll do!

Laura:
But Mother – I'm crippled!

Amanda:
Nonsense! Laura, I've told you never, never to use that word. Why, you're not crippled, you just have a little effect – hardly noticeable, even! When people have some slight disadvantage like that, they cultivate other things to make up for it – develop charm – and vivacity – and – *charm*! That's all you have to do! One thing your father had *plenty* of – was charm!

I CAPTURE THE CASTLE
BY DODIE SMITH (1948)

(Two sisters, Rose and Cassandra, live in a Castle. Rose is engaged to a young American man but does not genuinely love him. She is hoping his wealth may help to save the family home. Meanwhile, her younger sister, Cassandra, has developed feelings for him).

Cassandra:

I won't try to find out if Rose cares for him – what's the use? And I mustn't, I mustn't let her know about me. *(Rose enters)*

Rose:

Topaz is actually dancing across the courtyard. She gets more bogus every day.

Cassandra:

Yet somehow, she's genuine too. How mixed people are. How mixed nice. Oh, honeysuckle!

Rose:

Messy stuff. Simon stopped the car to gather me some.

Cassandra:

Rose! You don't love him.

Rose:

No. Pity, isn't it?

Cassandra:

Why did you lie to me the night you got engaged?

Rose:

I didn't. When he kissed me, it was – well, exciting. I thought that meant I was in love. You wouldn't understand. You're too young.

Cassandra:
I understand, all right. How long have you known?

Rose:
For ages. But it's got worse since I went to London – he's with me so much more there. Every minute we're together I can feel him *asking* for love. He somehow links it with everything – if it's a lovely day or we see anything beautiful. Oh, it's such a comfort to talk to you.

Cassandra:
Poor Rose. Would you like me to tell him for you?

Rose:
Tell him? Oh, I'm still going to marry him.

Cassandra:
You are not. You're not going to do anything so wicked.

Rose:
Why is it suddenly wicked? You helped me get him long before you thought I was in love with him.

Cassandra:
I didn't understand. It was just fun – like something in a book. It wasn't real.

Rose:
Well, it's real enough now.

Cassandra:
You can't do it, Rose – not just for clothes and jewelry.

Rose:

You talk as if I'm doing it all for myself. Do you know what my last thought has been, night after night? At least they've had enough to eat at the castle today. And I've thought you of you more than anyone – of all I'm going to do for you.

Cassandra:

Then you can stop thinking – because I won't take anything from you. And you can stop pretending to be noble. You're going to wreck his whole life. When he's the most wonderful person who ever lived...

Rose:

You're in love with him yourself. Oh, no! Darling, listen. I swear I'd give him up if he'd marry you instead. I'd be glad to because he'd still go on helping us. I don't want a lot of luxury – but I won't let us all go back to such hideous poverty. And we'd have to if I gave him up, because he'd never fall in love with you. He thinks of you as a little girl.

Cassandra:

What he thinks of me has got nothing to do with it.
It's *him* I'm thinking of.

Rose:

Do you realise what would happen if I broke the engagement? He'd let Scoatney Hall to the Fox-Cottons and go back to America with Neil. How would you like that?

Cassandra:

You're not going to marry him without loving him.

Rose:

Don't you know he'd rather have me that way than not at all?
(A motor horn is heard)

163

There's the car back. We'll talk again. I'm supposed to be staying at Scoatney tonight, but I'll say I want to be with you. We'll try to help each other.

Cassandra:

If you come back here, I won't speak to you. And I'm not coming to Scoatney. I'm not going to watch you show your power over him.

Rose:

But you must come. What'll they think if you don't?

Cassandra:

Tell him I have a headache!

Rose:

If you know how wretched I am…

Cassandra:

Go and make a list of your trousseau – that'll cheer you up. You grasping little cheat.

Rose:

You're failing me just when I need you most.

AUTHOR INDEX

As you Like It by William Shakespeare (1599)
Twelfth Night by William Shakespeare (1602)
Tartuffe by Moliere (1664)
The Rivals by R B Sheridan (1775)
The School for Scandal by R B Sheridan (1777)
The Way of the World by William Congreve (1700)
Little Women by L M Alcott (1868)
Lady Windermere's Fan by Oscar Wilde (1892)
The Importance of Being Earnest (1894)
A Month in the Country by Ivan Turgenev (1855)
A Doll's House by Henrik Ibsen (1879)
Hedda Gabler by Henrik Ibsen (1890)
Uncle Vanya by Anton Chekhov (1890)
Three Sisters by Anton Chekhov (1900)
The Cherry Orchard by Anton Chekhov (1903)
Mrs Warren's Profession by G B Shaw (1902)
Pygmalion by G B Shaw (1914)
Antigone by Jean Anouilh (1942)
A Streetcar named Desire by Tennessee Williams (1947)
The Glass Menagerie by Tennessee Williams (1944)
I Capture the Castle by Dodie Smith (1948)

ABOUT THE AUTHOR

Kim Gilbert trained as a professional actress at the Guildford School of Acting, studied for an LGSM with the Guildhall School of Music and Drama and took an English degree at the Open University. She has been acting, teaching and directing plays and musical productions for more than 35 years. She has experience in a wide range of theatre, TV and voiceover work. She has a First-class Honours degree in English and has taught English and Drama in many top schools in the country. Kim has examined for Lamda for a number of years and has also acted as an adjudicator. She has been running Dramatic Arts Studio for 11yrs, a private drama studio which specialises in developing excellence in all forms of performance and communication.

Other books by the same author

<u>Shakespeare Scenes</u>
Monologues for young adult female actors
Monologues for young female actors
Duologues for female actors
Monologues for young male actors

<u>Chekhov Scenes</u>
Monologues & Duologues for women
Monologues for Male Actors

<u>Scenes from Oscar Wilde</u>
Monologues for female actors
Monologues for Male actors
Duologues from Oscar Wilde

Classic Monologues for female actors
Classic Duologues for female actors
Classic Acting Monologues for Girls (8-14yrs)
Classic Acting Monologues for Boys (8-14yrs)
Classic Duologues for Boys & Girls (8-14yrs)

<u>Improve Your Voice</u>
How to speak English with confidence

Available from Amazon Bookstore

Thank you for reading! If you enjoyed this book or found it useful, I would be grateful if you'd post a short review on Amazon. Your support really does make a difference and I read all the reviews personally so I can get your feedback and make this book even better. Thanks again for your support!

Printed in Great Britain
by Amazon

67566201R00099